D1547355

# NO GREATER
# PAIN

# NO GREATER
# PAIN

## HOW TO HEAL WHEN YOUR CHILD DIES

*Surviving an unthinkable journey,*
*Embracing Grief and finding joy*

AUTHORED BY:
# RONALD J. ROSS

PALMETTO
PUBLISHING

Charleston, SC
www.PalmettoPublishing.com

NO GREATER PAIN
Copyright © 2023 by Ronald J. Ross

All rights reserved
No portion of this book may be reproduced, stored in a retrieval system, or transmitted
in any form by any means–electronic, mechanical, photocopy, recording, or other–
except for brief quotations in printed reviews, without prior permission of the author.

First Edition

Paperback ISBN: 979-8-8229-0860-4
eBook ISBN: 979-8-8229-0897-0

# TABLE OF CONTENTS

# DEDICATION

AMANDA ROSS — This book is dedicated to my daughter, who died on September 27, 2021.

I am a bereaved father who lost his loving daughter. Sweet Amanda was always concerned more for others than herself. Her charming, caring personality was infectious. She would give everything she had to anyone in need; her generosity was genuine and from her heart. Amanda searched for happiness throughout her life; she finally found it with her daughter, Ellie, who changed her life in the most positive way.

May God bless Amanda and hold her gently in His loving arms. She will be missed forever.

November 30, 1986 – September 27, 2021

# TESTIMONIAL

*The loss of a child is like no other. Unfortunately, it is a loss often misunderstood. If you know someone who has lost a child, remember that their "good" days are more complex than ever imagined. Remember that your worst day is still better than a bereaved person's best day. Compassion and love, not advice, are needed. My journey provides an inside look at why the loss of a child results in lifelong Grief. You will heal in time, but it takes much longer than expected; only those who have lost a child can understand that this journey will last a lifetime. This story is my honest reflection on love lost and strength gained.*

*By: Ronald J. Ross*

*Death leaves a heartache*
*no one can heal,*
*Love leaves a memory*
*no one can steal.*

# FOREWORD

THIS EXCERPT WAS written and published by *ABedForMyHeart. com*, © Donna Ashworth Words.

## — You Don't Just Lose Someone Once —

*You lose them over and over,*
*Sometimes many times a day.*
*When the loss, momentarily forgotten,*
*Creeps up*
*And attacks you from behind.*
*Fresh waves of Grief as the realization hits home:*
*They are gone. — Again.*
*You don't just lose someone once,*
*You lose them every time you open your eyes to a new dawn,*
*And as you awaken,*
*So does your memory,*
*So does the jolting bolt of lightning that rips into your heart:*
*They are gone. — Again.*
*Losing someone is a journey,*
*Not a one-off.*
*There is no end to the loss,*
*There is only a learned skill on how to stay afloat*
*When it washes over.*
*Be kind to those who are sailing this stormy sea,*
*They have a journey ahead of them,*
*And a daily shock to the system each time they realize*
*They are gone — Again.*
*You don't just lose someone once,*
*You lose them every day,*
*For a lifetime.*

# PREFACE

## WHY I WROTE THIS BOOK

I WROTE THIS book for several reasons.

First and foremost, I wanted to honor my daughter's legacy, to show how much her family and I love her. When you lose a child, your life changes dramatically; only those who have lost a child can truly understand the extreme pain and overwhelming Grief.

I want bereaved and non-bereaved parents to see the effects of Grief and this journey. It's an unforeseen road that can be devastating but, in the end, is survivable. This journey flips your world upside down. The bereaved parent knows all of this, and I wrote this book to show others that many of us have loved and lost to the greatest extent. There is no greater conceivable agony than losing a child, especially when it is unexpected; the searing pain will last longer than you ever imagined.

Finally, I wrote this book to survive my loss. It helped me move from a dark place to a world of appreciation and kindness. It's a rugged, challenging mountain to climb. It changes you as a person. But after you read this book, I hope you will see that by following your heart and doing what is suitable for you, you will come through this nightmare. This book is my journey, written so the memory of my daughter, Amanda, will not be forgotten.

My heart goes out to those bereaved parents and others who have suffered a significant loss. Life holds no guarantees. We are all destined to absorb losses in our life. The key to survival is accepting the path in front of us with passion, emotion, appreciation, and strength.

# PROLOGUE

THIS BOOK IS divided into mini-chapters for easier reading. I have opened up my life to share these vulnerable feelings with you. I am proud to have the strength to do so. There are over 150 emotions and feelings that a parent may endure after losing a child, most of which I experienced during my challenge to survive my daughter's death.

The reflections in the second part of this book are my thoughts, emotions, and decisions that brought me to a safe place to survive this difficult journey. You will see the pain and suffering subside slowly, even if you never believe it will. Writing this book was my way of grieving daily and helped me remember and appreciate all the good things about my child.

This book will also open the eyes of anyone who knows a bereaved parent and will help them better understand that we live in a shadow of sadness, but we are firm in our convictions and compassion toward others who have lost a loved one. We learn to accept our path and live a fruitful life in memory of our child.

God bless all of you who have suffered this tragedy. However, there is strength to be gained through the love for your child because love conquers all.

# INTRODUCTION

READ THIS BOOK from beginning to end and avoid jumping to the later chapters. Most bereaved parents experience many parts of this journey. You will gain the strength to survive each day and strive to find joy in your life again. The bereaved parent will read through these emotions and realize there is truth to all of this. The non-bereaved parent will wonder if all these emotions and pain are genuine. As you read this book, these emotions, challenges, and episodes of despair are real. If you are a father, you may hide and suppress many of these emotions, but in the end, there will be some regrets if you do. If you are a mother who has lost your child, you will experience all of this.

Your heart will mostly heal, but it will take time. Your heart will never completely heal. How could it? You have lost what is most precious to you. It helps to remember the happy moments. Your loved one would want you to remember the joyful moments. Remember the good times but allow yourself to grieve their loss. It is acceptable to grieve for months, even years; you decide what is best for you. Don't let anyone take your grieving time away from you. It is your heart and life; do whatever you feel is right.

Please read this book with compassion if you have not lost a child. The parent reading this book who has lost a child will understand the mountain of natural emotions and the journey to embrace. Embrace it for your child and pray you can enjoy life and experience joy again. The goal is to balance your sorrow with the heartwarming thoughts of your child. Your child would not want you to be sad forever.

# SUMMARY OF CONTENTS

## Part 1:

I share the actual daily, weekly, and monthly events and emotions during my first year. Some of the events are followed by *"Reflections"* as a follow-up one year later. Throughout the book, you will see how my thoughts have resonated, from daily accounts to my feelings about those difficult times the following year. *"Reflections"* are my feelings looking back at this journey to show you how you change as a bereaved parent.

Stay with me through the first six months and my first year, and you will see the results of Grief through my honest reflections on losing my child. You may experience many of these thoughts and emotions. Knowing what's ahead may help you deal with the unexpected. I've experienced real Grief and sadness as any parent would, and I share my mental and physical challenges in a world that becomes your new reality.

Have the courage to grieve and get through your most difficult times. The physical impact of this journey through Grief is honest, and this book summarizes how I stayed afloat and relatively healthy through the trauma. I experienced emotional meltdowns; several had a disabling effect. However, you learn to embrace the sorrow and realize that emotional episodes will be part of your future. You may have a compassionate family, and you try to lean on the love of your family. It is important to note that family, friends, and relationships change, and I share how they have changed and what to expect.

# PART 2:

I express my deep thoughts about Grief, mourning, and life in general in the second part of this book. I have a loving family and friends and share these experiences. My in-depth reflections focus on finding hope, experiencing complex challenges, and learning what path to take. Grief is all-consuming; your efforts to get well will have expectations, disappointments, and setbacks. I have detailed how I survived and started feeling semi-normal again. 'Normal' is a word that doesn't exist anymore because there is no way to feel normal again after you lose a child. You realize that you are a changed person, living in a different world without your child. It is an unimaginable situation, but there is hope.

I share my perspectives and thoughts about the future in my attempt to get well. Finally, I express the 14 most important things I've learned after losing my child. If you have lost a child, these thoughts will resonate deeply. If you have not lost a child, you will now understand how bereaved parents feel and their harrowing journey; there are many of us.

I conclude with final thoughts about my daughter. Thank you for reading this book. If you have loved and lost, this may change your perspective on what is most important in life.

# SYNOPSIS

## THIS IS GRIEF

*Please read this, then close your eyes and imagine it.*

*This synopsis is not about how my child died, but it will give you a vision of the emotions of Grief. Unfortunately, it is a dream that turns into a nightmare.*

Imagine you are about to run a one-mile race. The excitement is in the air. You are energized, focused, and ready to give your best effort. Then, as the race starts, you sprint out from the starting line. You are doing what you love to do; you run with passion. You are enjoying life, and it is beautiful. You feel strong and determined.

As you are running, someone up ahead is involved in a tragic accident. The person up the road was hit by a car and died instantly. You run by and see the accident. You see the unimaginable. It's your daughter who came to see your race. Your child, who loved you, came to see her dad run this race and embrace his passion. Your world has just turned upside down.

Now you are in a dream—no, a nightmare. You try to run, but your legs won't move. You are in slow motion. Everything around you is a blur. A searing pain rips through your body. Your mind can't believe what you just saw. Disbelief surrounds you.

In this nightmare, all the people around you are family and friends watching in the crowd. They are calling to you, but you only hear a muffled sound; your ears are ringing loudly. They are all reaching out to you to help but feel that you have died inside. Nobody can help you. The race has ended. You think that your life is over. Now you have to run. Get the shock out of your system. You run and run and run toward nothing.

Suddenly, it is not a one-mile race; it is a marathon. You are exhausted, dizzy, heartbroken, shaking from the shock, and you can't move. The world is spinning. You feel helpless and try to run toward your child. You get stuck, you fall, and you can't get up. Then it starts raining, and the rain is like the millions of tears that pour out of your eyes.

You start crawling and barely have the energy to stand up. It would help if you could get to your precious child. Finally, you start running again to get to your child, but the day turns into total darkness; you can't see anything. You are running and need to move forward, but there is no light. You are drained and exhausted. You can't get near your child. All you want to do is to see your child, hold your child one more time and at least say goodbye.

But you can't; it is too late. Sorrow consumes you. Now you are running down a lonely path in excruciating physical and mental pain. What do you do? You pray that this nightmare will end. You pray for strength, because you will never make it through life without your child. You hope that you will wake up and everything will be fine. But it's not okay; it was not a dream or a nightmare; it was real.

You have lost your child and your future with your child, and the sudden sadness and loneliness are debilitating.

**This is Grief!** It is most likely what every bereaved parent who has lost their child, no matter what their age or how they died, will experience. There is "*No Greater Pain*" to a human being than losing a child.

**This is Grief, and this is the unspoken truth.**

# PART 1

# AN UNEXPECTED LOSS

# CHAPTER 1

# LOSING A CHILD

LOSING A CHILD or a loved one unexpectedly, you know immediately that your life is changed forever. So when something like this happens, it shakes you to your core.

There is no getting over it; the only way forward is to manage through it. It's like driving into an unexpectedly dense fog on the road, and instantly, you can't see anything. You don't know how long it will take to make your way out of the fog; for long periods, you wonder if you will ever see the clear road in front of you again. Grief is the complex despair that sweeps through you like nothing you could ever imagine. You exit it as a different person when you have loved and lost so profoundly.

This is a story of my journey through Grief after losing my daughter. It is a shocking event when it is unexpected, and the trauma that follows is severe and debilitating. Putting words on paper allowed me to reflect on this most challenging journey. Many reflections are personal and address my honest insights into the unspoken truth about Grief. But if just one person reads this book, makes it through their Grief, and comes out of the fog on the other side to live again and find joy again, then this was all worth it. We will all experience Grief. It is inevitable, and when we love and lose, that Grief becomes authentic, deep, and, at times, unbearable.

I will carry the loss of my child forever.

Life goes on, and what was normal is not expected anymore. Through this trauma, you realize that you must own your Grief. This book encompasses all the emotional events, from the immediate shock and trauma of losing my daughter to the emotional roller coaster of experiences that followed. It isn't easy at times to read about these emotions. But please don't stop reading. A bereaved parent can overcome significant obstacles. I describe the challenges in the second part of this book. First, you realize there is no timeline for Grief to end; it ends if and when you are ready. The deeper you love someone, the deeper you grieve. And that is OK. It's healthy to grieve because you put aside your pride and allow yourself to experience the pain and suffering necessary to heal and forge ahead in life.

Will a bereaved parent be whole again? When there is an enormous emptiness the size of a crater in your heart, you can never close it completely. It will become your desire to carry it with you in a healthy way for the rest of your life; the love for your child or loved one will never diminish. Grief is a cross to bear. In this manner, those who have lost a loved one become more caring, compassionate, and changed in a good way. It is a long road. You can't suppress it; the journey grows longer if you do. There is hope and love for anyone who carries an open heart forward to family and friends.

You may no longer judge people because judgment is no longer in your heart when you lose someone special. When your energy is depleted, you only want to focus on positive, caring, and non-judging people. You will learn to avoid unhealthy situations that make your despair more profound. Instead, you desire to survive the day, the hour, and even each minute after learning of a love lost forever. I am not a doctor, a Grief counselor, or a Ph.D.

expert on Grief. My only expertise is my loss. In this loss, there is truth and honesty.

But this journey lets you see inside my world of Grief; it is a natural, honest journey, and it is my story. You experience the feelings and reactions of others that sometimes help you and sometimes do not. You come to realize that most people have good intentions.

Grief is something that can make people around you uncomfortable. But you have to own it, be strong, and embrace it because it is your love for your child or loved one, and no one can take that away. It is your life, your Grief, and in the end, your Grief will define you and strengthen you when you come out of the fog.

# CHAPTER 2

# THE EFFECTS OF GRIEF

GRIEF IS A word we occasionally hear, and in our culture, we think of it as a period of mourning over the loss of a loved one. But Grief is much more; it is the painful emotion that brings a human being to their knees.

Grief changes your world; it changes you as a person; it is a black hole you enter; initially, there is no light. Grief is misunderstood, especially for most men, who endure the cultural perception of being more resilient than women. But the reality is, male or female, Grief changes everything, crushing your spirit; you feel it will never go away. It is a scary, lonely, and painful heaviness to carry for the rest of our lives. You know that you will never be the person you once were, but you hope to persevere and find joy again. You look to your family and realize what you have; it provides relief. But Grief has broken your heart, and there are many pieces to pick up; you can't fix it with a Band-Aid. The emotional wound can't be closed or healed quickly; it must be managed and carried forward as part of you.

Grief changed my perspective on almost everything. Sadness was unavoidable and natural. When you grieve for a long time, maybe even years, the sadness may still live within you. It may become undetectable to those who know you, but it will always be with you—that inner sadness, your reminder of how much you love and miss your child.

If you have been sad and grieving for months, this is normal. So try to feel alive again and appreciate the things God presents to you. Anticipate that you may hear consoling statements such as: "You should appreciate and value what you have, and your child would want you to live life just as she did." Your family and friends are compassionate and have good intentions, but it doesn't make the Grief disappear. You realize your child is gone; your future with them has ended. Phone calls and video chats are gone. Birthdays and holidays will be difficult. But your memories and living life in their memory will not fade. You will always have your child in your thoughts and wonder why their precious life ended so soon.

Grief is a paralyzing emotion that everyone must endure. But losing a child is tremendous Grief; it is hell on earth. You never expected your child to die before you; this is the most challenging concept to accept. It shook my faith in God and made me wonder about my purpose in life.

Grief – I wouldn't wish this on anybody, and when I meet people with this same loss, there is an immediate emotional and compassionate understanding of their hardship. Grief goes deep into your soul; it must be endured by many. So many of us walk through the days in distress, and those who are fortunate to have not yet lost, may not realize the inner grief we carry inside; we can't keep telling everyone about our pain for months or years. Instead, we strive to live and experience joy again.

## SURRENDERING TO GRIEF

You will realize that you must submit to Grief and let the emotions flow. It is critical to getting well mentally and physically.

Your mental health will improve, and those negative emotions will turn positive. Initially, you believe that you can never survive this type of sorrow. You realize that you cannot suppress Grief or hold in your emotions because the love and sadness are too strong. So you climb the emotional mountain. Going it alone and thinking you can get through this tragedy is impossible. You want to withdraw, curl up and cry. You don't have the energy to see anyone; you're physically exhausted, and your emotional well-being can't bear it. It is best to surrender and grieve hard; allow no one to stop you. Grief is hard work; it slowly improves, though you may get stuck in it sometimes. You may grieve at the most unexpected moments and can cry instantly at the thought of your child. You may have emotional and mental meltdowns. There is not much difference between excruciating Grief and an emotional breakdown. To me, they are the same.

You believe there is a manageable future ahead. You find a way to embrace hope and endure the trying times that will come in 'waves' at the most unexpected times. Birthdays, anniversaries, and holidays are challenging, but there are ways to face these sensitive times and persevere. However, you may challenge your spiritual faith and question how you feel about your beliefs. It can be puzzling as you try to understand why this happened to your loved one. But, of course, you never expect to outlive your child; the 'order of life' doesn't make sense, but we have to live with that reality.

There is a path to remembering and rebuilding your life. Grief is ours to manage individually. There are ways to feel better but know this: You will always carry your child in your memory with everything you do; it will become a part of your life.

# CHAPTER 3

# MY FAMILY – THE BRADY BUNCH

*Except for my daughter's name, Amanda, and her daughter Ellie, names in this book are not included to protect the privacy of each family member, friend, and acquaintance.*

Amanda's mom and I were married for 12 years. I have since been remarried for 23 years, and my wife and I have raised our merged family of six children and six grandchildren, with another on the way.

My children and step-children are wonderful, and we have enjoyed family harmony during our marriage. Our adult children are close and caring for one another. Ellie is Amanda's three-year-old daughter. She brought happiness and comfort to Amanda and transformed her life. Ellie's father is Amanda's significant other, and his mother has been a loving grandmother to Ellie.

Grief is a difficult road to endure, and our family network is strong and caring, but the sorrow of losing Amanda took its toll on all of us. We are known as the Brady bunch, a family of three girls and three boys.

# AMANDA – My Daughter

Amanda was always warm and generous and had a heartfelt, charitable personality. She didn't care about having much money and was happiest when she went to the dollar store to buy small things for herself and Ellie. One day, working as a cosmetologist cutting hair, Amanda received 17 dollars in tips and was so thankful to receive these tips because her customers valued her—not a lot of money, but it meant the world to Amanda. She was very successful years prior, earning a good income, but it did not make her happy. Happiness was not money in her last years; It was Ellie, her beautiful daughter, who brought her joy. Amanda always thought of others and worried too much about family members, especially her mom and me. She always wanted to feel content that everybody was okay. Unfortunately, her anxiety would kick in with too much worry, often resulting in panic attacks.

Medically diagnosed with a social anxiety disorder, Amanda struggled to remain calm, reduce anxiety and not worry.

## Amanda's story about the homeless 20-year-old girl

Amanda was walking in the park with Ellie and came across a young girl, about 20 years old. She was crying, had torn clothing, and was frail-looking. Amanda sat with her and asked what was wrong. The girl said, "I'm homeless; my parents told me to leave their home. They told me that I was not welcome there anymore." Amanda asked, "How long have you been here? The girl replied, "I have been here for a day and a night; I am so thirsty and hungry."

Amanda took her to her apartment, not thinking of any danger, even though she had Ellie. She only wanted to help.

She prepared some food for the young girl: a sandwich, soup, and water. The young girl was appreciative. Amanda let her take a shower to clean up and gave her fresh clothes. She had no place to go, no food or money. Amanda drove her to the local food bank to show her where to get food for free. She also took her to the local soup kitchen, where a gracious staff served hot meals daily. Then she drove her to a homeless shelter and helped her check in, confirming that the girl could stay. She left her with fifteen dollars, giving her what she had. Amanda was a giving, loving person who always felt good about helping and being a caretaker for friends in any way she could. My daughter was so special; she had a heart of gold.

## Ellie – Amanda's 3-year-old daughter

Ellie is Amanda's little girl; full of laughter, playful, bright, and amazingly well-spoken for a three-year-old.

She will always come up to you if she thinks you are sad and hug you. She was the bright light that changed Amanda forever. Amanda became a great mom, and Ellie's personality reflects Amanda's cheerfulness; she is a sheer delight, full of energy. When it is time to go to sleep, she always wants to blow you a kiss, instilled precious bedtime memories from her mom. Now we will live our lives remembering Amanda through Ellie.

## ELLIE'S FATHER

Amanda was not married to Ellie's father. He had a difficult upbringing and lived with his stepfather, a critical figure in his early adulthood. However, he has proven that all he needed was a second chance to demonstrate that he could be a good father and person.

He returned to trade school to enhance his skills to become a barber. He worked as a cook and in construction during his earlier years. When his father and grandfather passed on, he received a modest inheritance and planned to support Ellie. Since Amanda's death, her mom had temporary guardianship of Ellie. We all intended to share in Ellie's care and upbringing.

We could tell how much he loved his daughter; his emotions would show his affection for Ellie when he visited. Amanda's significant other has a good heart. He loves Ellie tremendously and continues to be a hands-on father figure in her life. His mother has also supported and cared for Ellie and makes Ellie the center of her life.

# CHAPTER 4

# AMANDA'S MOTHER

## A Mother's Memory:

Amanda's mother provided this passionately written passage, published by Dr. Joanne Cacciatore and shared here with permission from both of them. The content captures her mother's feelings about our daughter and her love for Amanda.

As quoted:

*I am a parent. I am a bereaved parent. My child died, and this is my reluctant path. It is not a path of my choice, but it is a path I must walk mindfully and with intention. It is a journey through the darkest night of my soul, and it will take time to wind through the places that scare me.*

*Every cell in my body aches and longs to be with my beloved child. I may be impatient, distracted, frustrated, and unfocused on days when Grief is loud. I may get angry more quickly, or I may seem hopeless. I will shed many, many, many tears. I won't smile as often as my old self. Smiling hurts now. Most everything hurts some days, even breathing. But please, sit beside me. Say nothing. Do not offer a cure. Or a pill, or a word, or a potion. Witness my suffering. Please don't turn away from me. Please be gentle with me. And I will try to be gentle with me too.*

I will never "get over" my child's death, so please don't urge me down that path. Even when Grief is quiescent, when it isn't standing loudly in the foreground, even on days when I can even smile again, the pain is just beneath the surface. There are days when I feel paralyzed. My chest feels the sinking weight of my child's absence; sometimes, I feel like I will explode from the Grief. Losing my child affects me in many ways: as a woman, a mother, and a human being. It affects every aspect of me: spiritually, physically, mentally, and emotionally.

There are days when I barely recognize myself in the mirror anymore. Grief is as personal to me as my fingerprint. Don't tell me how I should or shouldn't be grieving or that I should or shouldn't "feel better by now." Don't tell me what's right or wrong. I'm doing it my way, in my time. To survive this, I must do what is best for me. My understanding of life will change, and a different meaning of life will slowly evolve. What I knew to be accurate or absolute, honest or fair about the world, has been challenged, so I'm finding my way, moment to moment, in this new place.

Things that once seemed important to me are barely thoughts any longer. I notice life's suffering more—hungry children, the homeless and the needy, a mother's harsh voice toward her young child—or an older adult struggling with the door. There are so many things about the world that I now struggle to understand: Why do children die? There are some questions I've learned which are simply unanswerable. So please don't tell me that "God has a plan" for me. This, my friend, is between my God and me. Those platitudes slip far too easily from the mouths of those who tuck their child into a safe, warm bed at night: Can you begin to imagine your child, the flesh of your flesh, lying lifeless in a casket when "goodbye" means you'll never see them on this Earth again?

*Grieving mothers, fathers, grandparents- and siblings won't wake up one day with everything 'okay' and life back to normal. I have a new normal now. As time passes, I may gain gifts, treasures, and insights, but anything gained was too high a cost when compared to what was lost. Perhaps, one day, when I am very, very old, I will say that time has truly helped to heal my broken heart.*

*But always remember that not a second of any minute of any hour of any day passes when I am not aware of my child's absence; no matter how many years lurk over my shoulder, don't forget that I have another one, another child, whose absence, like the sky, is spread over everything. As C.S. Lewis said ..."My child may have died, but my love - and my parenthood - never will."*

# CHAPTER 5

# LOSING MY DAUGHTER

I read several books about Grief and near-death experiences. My readings are provided at the end of this book. They offer hope and help you realize you are not alone; parents endure many tragedies. All these books can help a bereaved parent to persevere through the sadness and understand the stages of Grief. It is undeniably the most intense, heart-wrenching, and saddest time for anyone to endure. You experience shock, trauma, numbness, tears, fogginess, sadness, and loneliness at the loss of a loved one. Anyone who has lost a child goes through these complicated emotions that affect you physically and mentally, reaching levels that can be dangerous and unforgiving. These feelings are with you for a long time, but hopefully, as time passes, the intensity and frequency will lessen just a little so you can function again.

Accepting the death of your child is the most difficult, mind-numbing feeling to experience, and it was always the most complex feeling for me as I struggled to 'believe' what had happened.

You know that the hole in your heart may never go away, nor should it, because when you lose a child, the emptiness and sadness will carry on throughout your life. You have to manage it, but as any grieving parent would acknowledge, you never get over it.

It has been written, 'when you lose a parent, you lose the past. When you lose a spouse, you lose the present. When you lose a child, you lose the future.' That is the most challenging thing to accept because you lose all the future years that would have been. Writing this book helped me to cope with my most significant loss, so I could reflect on this someday and remember the challenges I embraced that led to my survival. I hope this book provides all grieving parents the strength to move forward with more kindness and understanding for others.

One of Amanda's favorite sayings is this:

**"In a world where you can be anything, be kind."**

## SURVIVING MY LOSS

The shock of losing a child—it's a mental trauma to your soul. When you first hear of your child or loved one's death, there is deep sorrow and unimaginable pain. The journey one must experience when losing a child is the most challenging time in a bereaved person's life. It involves all the complex emotions one can experience. It is a nightmare, and there is no sidestepping the anxiety, sleepless nights, and raw emotion that come with the death of your child.

There is raw emotion and unending tears for the first thirty days. After that, anger may set in, but persistent sadness is the most prevalent. Even with friends and family offering support and compassion, there is loneliness. You are not OK, and that's OK. Expect changes in your well-being. Initially, you are unfocused and confused; the daily suffering is overwhelming. But you allow yourself to surrender to Grief; it's necessary and best not to suppress it if you want to feel well again.

Stay with me on this summary. Ninety days sometimes feel like 90 minutes. When reality sets in, you feel numb with sadness, as if you'll never be happy again. Know this Grief because when you expect it, it's more manageable. Most people have told me, "I can't imagine what you're going through," and "I can't imagine how it would feel if I lost my child." They are correct. It may be difficult for one to imagine the searing pain of this kind of unexpected tragedy until it actually happens.

Through this journey, you'll see the many emotional mountains to climb: funeral arrangements, the viewing, the funeral service, and learning about what happened. You might question God and ask, "Why my child and not me?" You challenge the wrong order of life's events.

Your child was not supposed to die before you.

Many bereaved parents feel that part of them died when they learned of their child's death. You wonder who you are and how you'll live without them. It's still difficult to believe this has happened; it may take months to accept the reality of your loss.

# CHAPTER 6

# MY DAILY JOURNAL

## INTRODUCTION

This is my journey. It includes the hard times, the shock and trauma of a significant loss, the realization that your world has turned upside down, and that you are forever changed. But I have learned that through all the pain and suffering, there is hope—maybe not initially, but real hope of feeling close to normal again.

Some memories stay with you forever, and some result in unforeseen healing. In the end, you will live your life differently. However, you will always carry the fond memories of your child and learn to live again with resilience, knowing there will always be sadness in your heart.

I did not intend to sound dramatic regarding the first 30 days, weeks, and months following my child's loss. I toned down the emotions for this book. A non-bereaved parent may think the human emotions shared during these traumatic times seem unrealistic. A father, mother, and close-knit family will grieve deeply; tears are normal. However, the feelings and pain experienced by bereaved parents of children are a life-changing, life-altering event. So please read on, and you will see that there is hope: hope for healing, happiness, and your well-being.

## The beginning

My wife and I had just moved back to Maryland from South Carolina to be near family. We rented for nine months while we built our new home; it was an exciting time. My daughter, Amanda, had spent the last two years near us in South Carolina. Her mom lived close by and helped support Amanda and her three-year-old daughter, Ellie. In some ways, it was not easy leaving Amanda; we had such a close relationship.

My wife and I finally moved into our new home in mid-September; we were so happy and excited to be in our new home. Amanda had planned to visit several times each year. She was excited to see us for Thanksgiving and planned to spend extended time with us on her visits.

On September 27th, I set out to run an errand. A few miles from the house, I received a frantic call from my wife. What had happened? I had never heard my wife so upset. My world was about to turn upside down. There would be an emptiness, shock, and trauma in my heart that I could never have imagined.

# DAY 1

---

# WHEN YOU FIRST HEAR OF YOUR CHILD'S DEATH

## THE FIRST WEEK

## DAY 1

While I was driving, my wife called me on the phone and urgently pleaded, "Turn around; please come home immediately!" I asked, "What is wrong?" My wife only responded, "Please turn around and come home; please hurry." There was traffic; I was only two miles away, and five minutes seemed like an hour; something was terribly wrong, but she wouldn't tell me. The desperation in her voice was upsetting, and I thought someone had gotten hurt. My mind was racing with different thoughts. Was my wife hurt? Did something happen to one of our children? Did something happen to my in-laws? It seemed like an eternity to get home; I rushed into the house and saw my wife crumbling with despair. "What's wrong? Please tell me everything is fine. Is everyone OK? Please, God!" I pleaded to my wife as I began to fear the worst possible news.

My wife began to tell me the news, and her eyes welled up. Before she said a word, my heart started beating what seemed like a thousand times a minute. I never saw such a look of anguish; she could barely breathe the words. My wife told me that it was my precious daughter, Amanda. She said, "It's Amanda; she is gone." "What do you mean 'gone'?" "Amanda has passed," she said, crying. I let out screeching sounds that came from the core of my being. "Please tell me that she is not gone. NOT Amanda—what? Oh my GOD, NO! NO!! NO!!! NO!!!!" My wife collapsed into my arms. I sank to the floor and sobbed. "No, no, no, it can't be true. Please tell me she is not dead! It can't be true!"

My emotions were out of control. I just circled the room over and over again, screeching the words "No! No! No!" for what seemed like an eternity. Time seemed to stop.

"It can't be true! Not my Amanda!" More tears flowed in one hour than I have ever cried in a lifetime. I was hysterical, pacing throughout the room. My wife was crying uncontrollably, in the most intense despair and pain we had ever experienced. It was a hell I could never have imagined. I was bent over in inconceivable pain, so great that my body shook with emotion; it felt like my insides would explode. Your mind doesn't want to believe what you just heard. You can't comprehend the news of your child dying.

Everything seemed to be in slow motion, everything I heard sounded muffled, and everything was out of focus. It wasn't easy to breathe. I was in shock. I had lost my daughter; it crushed my spirit beyond my imagination.

### Reflection:

Looking back on this day after one year, I felt like I was in the twilight zone, unable to grasp the reality of what had happened. This shocking news was a nightmare that drew every breath out of my body. But any parent who has lost a child will remember that first day's microscopic details and the trauma that follows.

## DAY 2 - DISBELIEF

In the past, my wife and I had prayed that something like this would never happen to our children. The day after learning Amanda was gone, I sought to understand what had happened. We flew to South Carolina. My emotions were out of control, and my world was turned upside down. Tears continued to flow, and the shock was unbearable; it was constant disbelief and all-consuming, unimaginable pain. It was a living nightmare. My wife, emotional and distraught, tried to be comforting, but the shock was too much for us. We called the immediate family to give them the horrifying news. It was one hysterical moment after another; it was difficult to speak the words.

## DAY 3 - SHOCK

Amanda's mom picked us up at the airport, and we drove directly to our daughter's apartment. Walking into her place, her bedroom, and seeing the large picture of her and little Ellie, we all had a complete breakdown.

My mind turned toward trying to understand more about what happened. My former wife's husband found Amanda lying lifeless on the floor, cold and motionless. He called 911. Hearing him describe what he saw was crippling. Every breath was exhausting. Amanda's life was over; it destroyed my will.

That night, my wife and I slept in her apartment. Numb and distraught, we found sleep impossible. It was unbearable to imagine what had happened.

**Reflection:**

Those first three days for any parent are so incredibly challenging. During the first few days, you have hundreds of thoughts. There is no avoiding the traumatic, intense physical and emotional pain of a loving parent. You want to be with your child. Nothing else matters. Your mind cannot comprehend the shock of it all.

# Day 4 - Trauma - Dark Thoughts

So much emotional pain, a cloudy mind, body shaking, and never-ending tears—dazed by the shock, it isn't easy to speak. I spoke to the coroner and police investigating the case. It was highly confusing, as they mentioned there was no definitive cause. The apartment was swept and searched for clues; police found nothing to indicate the cause of death. The coroner could only tell me that Amanda collapsed on the floor. Three-year-old Ellie was alone with her mom; there was no one to call 911.

It was heartbreaking thinking about Ellie trying to wake up her mom.

Unfortunately, my thoughts turned dark and toward suicide; you want to die to see your loved one again. Never was I in a place so profoundly dark. I apologized hysterically to my wife and kept saying, "I am sorry." I apologized because, in my mind, the pain was unbearable. I wanted to die and leave this earth. My wife didn't respond, unsure why I was apologizing. You want your heart to cease beating to relieve the agony. You feel like a part of you has died. Extreme trauma and acute Grief make you feel as if you are free-falling from the sky with no parachute.

**Reflection:**

A year later, we learned that Ellie tried unsuccessfully to wake her mom up, so she decided to go to bed and sleep, thinking that her mom would be awake in the morning. Ellie sobbed uncontrollably and said, "I went to sleep and woke up; why didn't Mommy wake up like I did?" A three-year-old child remembers.

Regarding suicidal thoughts, when unexpected shock occurs, you want to end the searing, internal, unimaginable pain. You remember the disbelief; it becomes the darkest moment in a bereaved parent's life. You understand how people in this much pain could consider suicide. However, these thoughts do not last.

# DAY 5 - SADNESS

Our flight back to Maryland was full of sadness.

I tried to cope, to not get emotional, but I continued to feel numb. When you are in incredible, shocking pain, you want the aching to stop because you know the suffering will take its toll. It would alter my life forever. Landing at the airport, I wished the plane would crash.

It is a terrible feeling; you don't want to face the anguish ahead. With both of us shaking and emotionally unstable, my wife was unsure we would make it home safely. I drove like a zombie, trying to focus; everything seemed surreal. A bereaved parent cannot stop thinking about what happened. The pain ran so deep it was excruciating; I felt I couldn't breathe. It was a scary ride home.

## DAY 6 - DESPAIR

The despair continued. The thoughts of suicide passed, but I felt helpless. You have a shattered heart; nothing seems to matter anymore, even though you know you have a family that still depends on you.

I didn't want an autopsy for Amanda and pleaded to whoever would listen to avoid the terrible process. An autopsy is such an invasive procedure. I wanted my daughter's body to remain whole. Then panic set in, as I thought that Amanda might be an organ donor. The thought of an autopsy crushed me. Finally, the coroner informed us that no organs were viable since too much time had passed. However, by law, he had to complete an autopsy because the death of a thirty-four-year-old was suspicious.

### Reflection:

Looking back at the thought of an autopsy, parents have the difficult decision to avoid it or to help someone else in need. I wanted to remember my daughter whole. The heartbreak of having my daughter's body go through the terrible process of an autopsy was unimaginable.

# Day 7 – Coroner's Report – Amanda's obituary

The coroner completed his report. He found nothing. There were no blood clots, brain bleeding, heart attack, injuries, or criminal evidence. The coroner submitted blood and tissue samples for a toxicology report to a lab. The testing and information would take three months.

There were no immediate answers.

I had to write Amanda's obituary. What parent would ever think they'd have to do this? So I thought, *How can I do this?*

How could I write my daughter's obituary? No parent should have to write an obituary for their child; it goes against every regular order of life. No one should ever have to outlive their child. But I did what was necessary. The words flowed effortlessly because saying all the beautiful things about Amanda was easy.

### *Reflection:*

When the coroner found no immediate cause of death, I still remember my extreme anxiety. Waiting for answers seemed like time had stopped. As a bereaved parent, these are the sad thoughts you try to avoid and instead focus on happy memories to heal. The obituary is something no parent ever desires to write. It is an unreal time. You write about your child who is lost forever. I barely remember that day.

# CHAPTER 7

# THE HEARTBREAKING FUNERAL

## DAY 8 – FUNERAL ARRANGEMENTS

Arranging a funeral for my child—the details, the decisions, and the checklist—it's surreal; the process is numbing. My family helped me tremendously. Without their support, I don't know if I could have survived the day. The gentleman at the funeral home stepped through the funeral arrangements like a used car salesman, item by item: casket, flowers, upgrade options, gravesite—it was appalling. We couldn't help but notice his indifference and matter-of-fact demeanor. Finally, my wife called him out on his insensitivity, reminding him that we had just lost our daughter unexpectedly 24 hours earlier. It might be just another day at the office for him, but it was excruciating for us. She requested another coordinator to guide us through the remainder of the funeral. We had him replaced. The sadness consumed both of us.

## DAY 9 - PREPARING TO SEE AMANDA

My family pulled together hundreds of photos of Amanda, capturing her lifetime memories with all of us. Realizing you'll never talk to or see your child again is the saddest and loneliest feeling. The thought of seeing my daughter at the viewing created great anxiety; I prayed that she would look just as I last saw her. As a parent, seeing your child lying in a coffin is crippling; it destroys your heart. The day was unfocused and numbing. I was distraught beyond words; my body shook in despair and deep emotional pain. There was no sleeping that night, and exhaustion was insurmountable. I prayed for strength, and, at that time, felt incredible weakness leading up to the day of the viewing

God, give my family and me the strength to make it through these next two days. God bless my Amanda. Rest in Peace; we will love and miss you forever.

## DAY 10 – THE VIEWING

Driving to the funeral home for the first private viewing of my daughter was an emotional challenge. I couldn't see Amanda before this day, as she died in South Carolina. After much co-ordination between the coroner and the funeral home, we flew her back to Maryland. So many things went through my mind; I feared the worst. Arriving at the funeral home parking lot, I saw my son coming out of the building. I asked him if Amanda looked as I remembered her.

You never forget these moments; he shook his head no. Grief overwhelmed me. Time stopped; uncontrolled anxiety, sadness, and anger consumed me. I felt dizzy and began to collapse. My son held me up. Seeing my precious daughter lying in that coffin changed my life forever.

However, family and friends visited for two days, many that I hadn't seen in years. Seeing the outpouring of love was heart-warming, but it was exhausting.

**Reflection:**

It was a time never to be forgotten. The funeral arrangements, preparing to see your child lying in a coffin, and the actual viewing are the most indescribable painful feelings. A year has passed, and the thoughts of those problematic days stay with me. I don't dwell on these thoughts a year later because they can lead to long-term depression. Bereaved parents must find the strength to remember all the good moments in their child's life.

# DAY 11 – THE FUNERAL

We decided on a private funeral for immediate family and guests. The pastor preached with positivity and assured us there was peace ahead for Amanda. That helped some, and I felt at ease that Amanda had found her faith, which was vital. At the final viewing, as we said goodbye to Amanda one last time, the grad-uation song "Friends Forever" was played; it was heartbreaking. Amanda and all our family were "friends forever," with love. I spoke at the funeral.

I saved a voice message from Amanda on my phone and wanted everyone in the room to hear Amanda one last time.

Her message was full of love.

*She said, "Hi Daddy, I just wanted to call you to say I love you and miss you, and I feel so grateful about my life. I worked to-day and earned 17 dollars from tips, making me happy. So I just wanted to say I love you and can't wait to see you in July".*

Tears filled the quiet room. It was a precious moment to hear Amanda's voice and share it with all my family. I spoke to everyone in the room:

> When you talk to your child, your parents, or your siblings, remember to say I love you because you never know if that might be the last time you speak. Tomorrow is not guaranteed to anyone.

We have all heard these words at some point. At that moment, I prayed that Amanda was looking down at us, bonded together in our love for her.

We decided to have a wake at our new home after the funeral; it was almost empty of furnishings, just as all our hearts were empty that day. Everyone was gracious, helpful, and caring. Our children and extended family coordinated the catering, a generous gift at the time.

# DAY 12 – REALITY SETS IN

Reality began to set in the day after the funeral, and the Grief grew stronger. My family stayed over, and their support helped me stay calm. Waking up and realizing that it's over, that you will not see your loved one again, creates a permanent hole in your heart. You feel increased sadness; you question everything. What could you have done to prevent this? You feel anger toward God. Why take a life that was starting with her newfound faith? You convince yourself that God took your child because He wanted another angel in heaven. She was committed to the Lord. That helped me get through some of the pain.

My decision to reserve a cemetery plot beside Amanda was on my mind. I wanted to be lying beside my daughter for my final resting place. It was a big decision, but for me, it was right. You want to live life but, for the first time, feel at total peace about dying. You accept that your time will come. I would have a resting place, which brought me peace. It would help me through the suffering and give me the strength to move forward.

## Reflection:

Attending your child's funeral changes how you look at all funerals. A year later, when I attended a funeral, it resonated deeply, and the sorrow and sadness for that individual emerged. You get these reminders about your child's funeral, which recreates that unavoidable anxiety.

Just as a bereaved parent remembers the painful process of coordinating the viewing, seeing the coffin, and going through the funeral with weakened legs, all funerals will trigger those emotions. You remember how you survived each day, and you learn to be much more compassionate to those who have lost a loved one. It is natural and automatic.

## Day 13 - Anxiety

There was a strong desire to see my child's grave soon after the funeral. Some bereaved parents cannot revisit the cemetery so quickly, but this was my desire. I purchased fresh topsoil, a watering can, and grass seed at a local store. I brought a ceramic angel that was a gift from my stepson. I tidied the area at the cemetery, placed the angel beside her picture, and watered the new lawn over her grave. Seeing lawnmowers sweep through the graveyard caused me to worry that the flowers and angel would be damaged. You are so sensitive that you don't want any further harm. It doesn't make sense, but you become susceptible to everything. My visit was a quiet one. I didn't pray or speak; I just sat there in peace. There is an unwanted, unbearable pain that you feel will never end.

My wife, stepson, and I went to the theater to see the James Bond movie *No Time to Die*. Believe it or not, that was the name of the film. I watched the movie, thinking this was no time for my daughter to die. My body shook for two hours, fighting back the tears during the movie.

That night and every night, you hope for a dream to be able to talk to your loved one and see them again. The dream never came. As anyone would, a bereaved parent yearns for that sign to validate that their child is safe.

# DAY 14 – QUESTIONING GOD, FEELING NUMB

My stepson flew back home to California, and the house was silent. Sitting alone was difficult; I thought about things I could have done differently.

The days seemed so long, the hours passed so slowly, and the clock seemed to stand still; it was torture. You wonder why God gives us tragedies. You wonder why He takes good people away and allows evil people to live. A bereaved parent will question the order of things for sure.

I began reading books on Grief and parents who lost their children. To better cope, reading was my outlet. It was essential to manage my emotions for my marriage to survive. My marriage was strong, but you know you are different from now on, though you don't know what kind of person you will become. The emptiness runs deep with a loss like this.

The days pass numbly. Constant images in your mind draw you into a depression so intense you feel you can't fight it; it is easier just to let it happen. It was caringly mentioned to me to avoid slipping into a deep depression. You wonder how that would even be possible.

It is unbearably hard to endure when you love your child and realize you can never see or talk to them again.

The sleepless nights for a bereaved parent are lengthy. I would wake up at night not knowing if it was 1 am, 5 am, or 7 am. You continue to pray for a dream so you can have one last word with the hope of seeing and feeling your child one last time. But these wished-for dreams eluded me.

*Reflection:*

After a year, you will continue to experience sporadic sleepless nights. However, they are not as frequent and do not result in as many emotional private meltdowns. Within two weeks, I decided to write a memoir. First, I started a daily journal, converted it into a memoir, and decided to publish this book. Even though it was emotional writing throughout the year, it was my outlet to survive the days. Many studies encourage writing to manage acute Grief and mental trauma. A bereaved parent keeps hoping for that unique dream and does not lose faith. This dream will come when the time is right.

## THE EXPRESSION – "I CAN'T IMAGINE"

I heard these three words from many people at the viewing and the funeral. "I can't imagine." I remember saying these exact words to friends who lost their child in recent years.

My wife and I discussed how we hoped nothing like this would ever happen to any of our children. But now, our world was turned upside down. As I tried to pick up the pieces, I thought of a former friend who lost two sons to suicide. How did she survive?

Another friend lost his son to a violent act of unintentional manslaughter. He shared his thoughts on how he coped and survived the days after his son's death. Reaching out to a friend who has experienced loss, just as you have, helps you understand what to expect. My bereaved friend explained that it is a permanent mark in your heart that you carry for the rest of your life. But, he said, there is hope, and you learn to live through the memories of your child. His honesty and sharing of personal thoughts about life without his child were heartwarming.

Life holds no guarantees; indeed, there are no guarantees that tomorrow will come. Unfortunately, the unimaginable happens when you least expect it.

"I can't imagine." I have always heard it, and I have said it. Death makes everyone think, *What if this happened to me?* Parents who have not lost a child try to imagine the travesty of their child dying before they do. Unfortunately, it is not the normal process of life when your child dies before you do.

## GOD NEVER GIVES YOU TOO MUCH TO HANDLE

"God never gives you too much to handle."

When my child died, this statement made no sense. But unfortunately, some families feel the presence of death and experience great hardship, emotionally and physically. Events in my life were challenging; I was dealing with so many issues that it would take a chapter to explain. With my parents' deaths, divorce, child separation, chronic illness, and Grief in the family, I already felt God had given me too much to handle. But now, the death of my child?

In my earlier years, my parents' deaths were difficult to comprehend, especially when the second parent died, and I felt like an orphan. No parent to lean on during difficult times. They were ill for years, but because of that, we were more prepared for their passing. In hindsight, while you may feel extreme Grief when your parents die, you learn there is no more incredible pain than your child dying unexpectedly.

Your mind knows it, but your heart doesn't accept it. It took many months for me to acknowledge this truth. Your mind protects you from mental stress when you cannot accept that your child is really gone.

# CHAPTER 8

# FEELING BROKEN

## Days 15 – 21

When you experience intense grieving, everything is a blur, like a dense fog. You become forgetful, misplacing your keys, wandering from room to room, and staring at nothing. As each day passes, you barely remember the day before. All I could remember was when my wife told me Amanda was gone. I replayed that moment repeatedly; I couldn't get it out of my mind.

When I visited the cemetery, there were no words, just staring at the sky, wondering what had happened. Did Amanda suffer when she collapsed? Was she struggling to call 911? It was excruciating to think about these things, and I hoped to get answers with the toxicology report. Three months to wait for the results—it would feel like three years.

## DISBELIEF CONTINUES

Early every morning, sadness returns; it saps your desire to get out of bed. So I would make coffee, lots of it, to try to get some energy. Living in a rural area surrounded by farms, I'd sit on the back porch, staring at the corn fields, and my thoughts always turned to Amanda.

I felt ready to try to find 'normal' again. It was time to search for a headstone. Searching for a monument is an upsetting experience. There seems to be a lack of compassion when dealing with people. Everything seemed overpriced, but researching for a gravestone was a new and unwanted experience. I could not find the heart-shaped headstone I desired. It was enough for one day; the agony of this process becomes too much to bear during the early days of Grief.

## FAMILY AND FRIEND RESPONSES

Amanda's mom was devastated and broken. She gave all her love to Amanda, helping her raise Ellie and spending all her free time with her in South Carolina.

I have three siblings; my brother and two sisters. My older brother phoned. His sorrow was genuine and so sincere. Our conversations were emotional and tearful. He was hurting; my daughter's death affected him in many ways.

My sisters called to check on me and offer some comfort. They would occasionally call later on to provide sincere compassion. My sisters have love in their hearts. Everything is magnified when you are grieving.

A longtime friend stopped by to visit. A kind man, he is compassionate, as is his wife. We talked; he listened, offered help, and invited me to his Bible group. I preferred to grieve privately rather than fall apart at a Bible study. Maybe later, my mind would change. I tried to stay strong during his visit, but when he left, I broke down. My wife provided comfort and was always there, trying her best to support me, even in her Grief, for I knew how much she loved Amanda.

Friends called and texted, offering their support. Words are nice from caring and compassionate friends, but the despair continues even with the help of others.

## Raw Emotion

How does a person survive the worst possible loss and live to tell about it? Bereaved parents have intense, profound, dark moments of complex thoughts. You can get stuck in deep despair forever; it's a challenging loneliness to describe.

Over time, raw emotion becomes more sporadic and less constant. Then, finally, you feel relieved to get a break from crying's physical toll. A parent who dearly loves their child would give up their life in a second if they could trade places with their child. Most parents feel this way. It becomes real when it happens.

Men are "supposed" to deal with loss, support their spouse, not talk about their emotions, not lose control, and if they must cry—do so in private. But that wasn't me. So it wasn't easy to socialize or participate in family events, but my family was very understanding.

## What Happened?

After 20 days, the despair of a bereaved parent will affect you physically. I didn't recognize my reflection in the mirror; I looked broken and felt broken.

That is the truth, although it caused me little concern; at the time, I didn't care whether I lived another day. You can experience new ailments from the stress. I had a heart murmur that magnified itself from the stress. Sometimes you hope your heart will stop so you can be without pain finally. Not a healthy thought, but it was true.

Every bereaved parent desires to understand what happened to their loved one. I needed to focus on what happened to my daughter. She just collapsed, fell to the floor, and died. So many things went through my mind. What happened?

## LOST FUTURE

When you lose a loved one, it is not just losing them in the present, but you lose future memories of what life could have been.

Realizing that I would never see my daughter raise her child through all her life events just brought more sadness.

Birds would fly over our home every morning, forming a V-shape. Amanda loved birds, so I visualized the birds spelling out the letter 'A' for Amanda. We all look for signs; we never know if they are natural or coincidental. The desire to have that dream is constant. Of course, when so distraught, you wish for one more talk and to hold your child just one more time. You pray every day for this opportunity.

**Reflection:**

A year later, the feeling of a lost future with my child remained as a hole in my heart. How could it not? Reminders of what you have lost stay with you forever. Some family members provided caring support constantly. Others disappeared. The disbelief and raw emotion subsided after I learned the cause of my daughter's death. However, the loneliness and sadness continued well into the second year. It is normal to have lasting emotions as long as you do not enter deep, debilitating depression.

# CHAPTER 9

## MANAGING EMOTIONS

### DAYS 22-30

After four weeks, meltdowns were becoming unhealthy; it was time to stay calm. You try to keep yourself busy; your emotions need a break. There may not be a fundamental difference between grieving and suffering, and it became unhealthy prolonging it.

### SUFFERING DAILY

When you lose a child, you suffer. You decide to either suppress your emotions or give in to sorrow. In the mornings, the weight of another day overpowers the need to rise for another day.

When you search for serenity and calmness, you may do things that set you back. For example, I watched Amanda's 'good morning' videos to start my day.

Was I making myself grieve harder? Looking back, I was. Listening to one of her favorite songs played at the funeral, 'The Graduation song-Friends forever,' brought on a flood of tears. My wife could hear me, but she let me grieve privately. Sometimes, seeing me suffer, she would be overwhelmed by her own Grief.

*Reflection:*

It is essential to save any videos or audio messages from your loved one. It may be painful initially, but you will be grateful to have them after time has passed. With the advances in social media, you can save the fond memories of your loved one. Seeing and hearing your child's voice has enormous benefits to healing after that critical first year. For example, I kept videos of Amanda saying good morning, just brief hellos, good nights, or a short video of Ellie, and I was grateful to have them. Valuable memories like this become precious; you will keep them forever.

## READING BOOKS, LOOKING FOR ANSWERS

Reading helped me cope, and writing was my outlet. So I would rush to the computer and continue to write about all the struggles I experienced.

I read two books. The first is titled *Shattered*, and the second, *It's OK not to be OK*. Both books were excellent. I was starting a third book, *When a Parent Loses a Child*.

These books help you to understand the sadness, regrets, guilt, and pain. Initially, it didn't make a difference when friends and family reached out with condolences and support. The Grief created such a hollowness that even kind condolences did not alleviate the pain. You learn that these feelings are normal. And the fact is, receiving compassion and support from family and friends does help.

# I'm not OK

You know that you are not OK because you have never experienced the loss of emotional control over months of extended time. This is best summarized in the book, *It's OK not to be OK*, chapter eight, *How (And Why) to Stay Alive*. This excerpt describes what a bereaved parent experiences with the death of their child.

To quote the reading:

> Grief takes a toll on your mind, body, relationships —everything. The thought of endless months and years without the one you love is overwhelming. The thought of everyone else returning to their lives while you're still sitting in the wreckage is devastating. The reality is just too big to let in. For many people, continuing to wake up each morning is a disappointment. "Damn, I'm still alive."
>
> Thoughts like this make sense when Grief is so deep. Feeling you'd rather not wake up is normal. However, not wanting to be alive is not the same as wanting to be dead. You don't want to die but don't want to live. Bereaved parents feel like they are going crazy because they confuse their thoughts about life and death. Sometimes you don't care whether you live or die, not because you are suicidal, but because it no longer matters.
>
> It's difficult to explain that, as people understandably get upset when someone speaks of not wanting to be alive, so we stop talking about it.

Encouragement from others that you still have much to live for feels extraneous. You can't cheerlead yourself out of the depths of Grief.

So you hope that someday you will be 'ok,' but with the reality that the sadness will always be there. It's impossible to be the person you were before you lost your child; you realize you must accept your new normal.

For instance, during a tooth-pulling procedure in the dentist's office, I recalled that Amanda had dental work done just before she died. Some tears fell down my cheek. The dentist became alarmed and asked if she was hurting me. I assured her it was ok but didn't explain my thoughts. She didn't know about my loss, and there was no need to say anything. You learn that you don't have to tell everyone about your tragedy. It's an excellent way to shield yourself.

**Reflection:**

After considerable  time, you realize that everyone has moved on with their life. It is the way life works. Yes, you have the wreckage to carry, but you begin to accept and not become overwhelmed with the hair-trigger emotions you experienced in the earlier days. Time doesn't heal, but time lessens the overwhelming emotions. Your body cannot continue to be so exhausted that it debilitates you for years.

## Unfocused and Confused

Everything slows down; simple things become complicated. You become forgetful, unfocused, and slower to react. You can't seem to comprehend the simplest things. For example, we purchased a file cabinet that required assembly. The estimated time to complete it was sixty minutes. After reading the directions repeatedly, making dumb mistakes, and working aimlessly, I finished it four hours later. The time seemed to pass quickly, so the good news was that four hours had passed, and it was closer to nighttime to sleep away my Grief. Another piece of furniture only took me three hours to assemble, and my focus was improving. Not really—the Grief was still exhausting, and the sorrow was still raw.

You may find yourself watching television and turning it off because you don't even know what you are watching. Sitting for long periods, staring at nothing, not moving—the unwelcomed pain is so intense, your mind goes blank.

## Accepting your loss

You realize you may never get back to 'normal.'

How could you? What is your new normal? People change based on life experiences and grow differently, but how does one grow and change after a child's death? It is beyond comprehension.

I've read that it can take years to get through an unexpected loss. Years? After one month, the thought paralyzed me. How would I recover? It was daunting to think that this pain would always be with me.

**Reflection:**

As a father, there is a feeling of insurmountable Grief, which is seen as a weakness when there is extensive emotion. The notion that a man should be strong and suppress his feelings comes from our cultural upbringing. There is no timetable for the sorrow to recede; the closer you are to a child, the longer it will take to heal.

## GETTING HELP WITH MEDICATION

As you struggle with Grief, you start thinking about getting help. You begin to accept medicine to help you sleep. As you gain strength, you try to be normal and less emotional.

If you experience physical shaking, your despair will lessen over time. Eventually, your mind and body will give you some relief. However, if the shaking doesn't end, there can be a medical reason. The advice is to see a doctor. I decided to see a doctor after 90 days of constant shaking, especially at night.

With an unexpected loss, your internal drive might disappear. You decide that an antidepressant may help to provide some energy. Even after almost a month, being sociable and seeing extended family was still difficult. When people asked how I was doing, I was unsure how to respond.

## OTHER REACTIONS

If you have other children, it is crucial to support them. I would reach out to my son; he gave me space to grieve. He's very insightful, even as he deals with his own health issues. My son understood the importance of managing emotions.

My other daughter returned from a Christian retreat. She looked well and turned toward her faith. They organized a memorial for

Amanda. She mentioned she just wanted to receive a sign that Amanda was safe, happy, and in heaven. They enjoyed a favorite Christian song that they would sing together. On the way back from her retreat, she turned on the radio, and there it was: Their favorite song was playing. They talked about that song before she died. Hearing this song was a sign, maybe for real or perhaps a coincidence,

My wife was exhausted but seemed to find a way to function. Unfortunately, she had difficulty sleeping and was constantly under the weather. Grieving for Amanda significantly weakened her immune system. I never saw her so weakened and felt terrible. Grief takes everything out of you.

Amanda's mom was in South Carolina clearing out Amanda's apartment, getting her car ready to sell, and still looking for answers or clues about how she died. Working full time, she cried from 8 pm to 10 pm every day; it was the only time in her busy day to grieve. I imagined the busy schedule kept her from crumbling all day.

**Reflection:**

Reflecting on those early months, I realized that the mind and body protect you from the unexpected mental and physical trauma you experience. You are in a fog; you are unfocused and confused as you try to accept your loss, which seems unacceptable at the time. So considering medication is a normal desire. It helped me through the exhaustion. Grief does sap your strength. Remember, there is hope, but there is a need to eat, exercise, stay active, relax by taking walks, and be alone to grieve when necessary. It will take months or longer. Know that your mind and body are protected when you experience unexpected trauma.

Be patient and kind to yourself, even during the suffering stage of Grief.

## "Go Fund Me" donations

When Amanda died, her mother set up a "Go Fund Me" site for Ellie. There was a flood of donations, over 115 contributions. Amanda would have been pleased. The gifts from friends, family, and acquaintances were heartwarming. The future held no guarantee as to who would raise Ellie, as her father could not support her at the time. He was working toward rebuilding his life. We all prayed that Ellie's father would raise her in a good home environment.

After Amanda's funeral, he began to make restitution for the past. We believed and prayed he would succeed because it would be challenging for us, as grandparents, to raise a three-year-old child.

## Grieving for her best friend

Amanda had a strong bond with her lifetime best friend. Her friend was a single mom with three young children. Amanda would bring Ellie to her house, and the children would play all day. I speak in the past tense because Amanda's best friend died two years ago. She died on her birthday, succumbing to pills and alcohol while celebrating. It was an accidental overdose. Amanda did not want to be tempted and did not attend that party; she wanted to be safe with Ellie. Amanda continued to grieve the loss of her best friend for two years; she missed her terribly. It makes you realize that Grief has its own timetable. When Amanda died, it was close to the date that her friend died.

What is sadly ironic is that Amanda was always worried about her family. Whenever I talked to her, she asked how we were doing and often said it would be difficult to be happy if something happened to anyone in our family. Even though Amanda experienced physical issues, she never complained and didn't want her family to worry. If we were OK, then she felt OK.

## *Reflection:*

During the past year since Amanda's death, I have lost some friends and have received heartbreaking news from other friends. You become ultra-sensitive and emotional when you have lost a child. You wish for everything to stay the same. You hope friends and family stay well. But change can occur rapidly at times in your life. You have to expect that everything won't stay the same. Life changes, people become ill, and friends die. A bereaved parent will have that higher level of intense emotions only because they have been through the extreme mental and emotional trauma of losing a loved one.

# CHAPTER 10

# FIRST AND SECOND MONTH

## THE FIRST MONTH CHANGES YOU FOREVER

Many bereaved parents experience extended Grief. Families deal with sibling issues, divorce, parental death, and family illness. But losing a child brings a parent to their knees. It becomes too much to bear and results in severe mental pain and unrelenting despair. You want to live another 20 years, but it is difficult to imagine the same level of happiness as before your child died. My attitude changed dramatically; I was no longer fearful of death and ready to meet God to end the pain. But I intended to live, prepared to accept the end of God's journey for me in His time.

After 30 days, a bereaved parent remains in disbelief that their child is no longer alive. You fear you'll remain in this same place in the following months.

You feel like you might explode, unsure about handling anything, feeling numb and sad. You feel unhinged, and you get easily confused. Your mind becomes cluttered and disorganized, and you forget the simplest things. You have difficulty sleeping, and there is constant sadness. Finally, you fall into that known fourth stage of Grief, "early depression."

*Reflection:*

As I read these beginning chapters a year later, it seemed excessive and deep with raw emotions. Please keep reading. The days and months get better. Looking back, yes, you may have these very early extreme emotions due to the trauma, but there is relief in the future. You have to believe that life eventually becomes bearable.

# THE SECOND MONTH
## TRYING TO SURVIVE EACH DAY

In the second month, you try to regain your senses and normalcy. Unfortunately, it doesn't seem to get any easier; the feelings of emptiness and the sleepless nights still exist. Feeling guilty about many things, as little or significant as they may be, you try to manage your Grief.

One way to do so is to spend time grieving alone; solitude allows time to think and process without interruption. Finding joy in engaging in activities and having company for a short time can be challenging. It's exhausting to have visitors and socialize; it takes energy.

If you are married or have a significant other, the relationship becomes stressful, with each partner trying to navigate their way.

Reality begins to set in, and you think, *Is she really gone?* You never prepare for this, and the mental and physical pain is much greater when unexpected. So you suppress your Grief to try to move forward. But I am here to tell you that this doesn't work; it just prolongs the inevitable. You have to grieve.

## Continued Journey

The following chapters discuss my second 30 days.

Different feelings lead to more awareness. You begin to question everything, but your emotions lessen as you settle into your new 'normal.'

## Trying to Regain Normalcy

You need to start getting well and try to make it through the day without being overwhelmed with thoughts of sadness for your loved one. I experienced setbacks because there were no answers on Amanda's cause of death. You question everything in your mind. I wanted to find some answers; none of this made sense.

Questioning everything is normal when there are no answers.

It takes its toll mentally and physically. Gathering facts leading up to Amanda's death, my thoughts wandered; some were scary. Did she suffer? Was she in pain? For how long? Who might want to hurt Amanda? It was heart-wrenching. I hoped to get some answers because it was difficult to imagine moving on without knowing what had happened.

My wife and I talked about everything. She observed behavior that made her worry about my mental state, especially depression. I *was* depressed. How could I not be? Of course, you try to avoid sinking into a more profound depression. But to me, everything was still fresh and raw.

We were going to see Ellie soon. Seeing your grandchildren or other children can provide some joy for a bereaved parent. Her birthday was approaching; she would be three years old. We explained to her, with the guidance of a child psychologist, that her mom's heart was broken and that it couldn't be fixed; she would not be able to see her again. It brought more finality to the mind of a three-year-old. Mentioning Heaven and her being in a better place was not the best approach. A child may expect to see her mom in Heaven but is too young to understand the concept of Heaven. We told Ellie her mom loved her but would be forever gone. It was too heartbreaking for all of us.

## EMPTINESS

Your tears will stop for a while; you believe your tear ducts are finally dry. Your heavy heart carries a feeling of numbness. It physically hurts, it feels tight, and you may feel shortness of breath and chest pressure never before experienced. There is a constant feeling of emptiness. There is no doubt that a part of you dies with the loss of a child.

Many books have been published stressing that you can't get over Grief; you must get through it. You don't get by it because you can't get around it. It doesn't get better; it just gets different.

Every day, your Grief will have a new disguise.

I received a special heartfelt card from a friend. It stated:

> While the rest of the world carries on as though nothing has happened, remember that others know your world will never

be the same. And day after healing day, when you might think people have forgotten, we'll still be caring about you.

## BIRTHDAYS

No doubt, the nights continue to be difficult for a bereaved parent. At night one's mind goes into full gear, with thoughts that wear on your emotions. As a parent, when your birthday approaches, you may feel that you do not deserve to celebrate another year of life.

Since my daughter's birthday celebrations have ended, I felt comfortable not celebrating my birthday; it results in a sad reminder. Yet you desire to get through each day better than the day before.

Celebrating your child's birthday is painful for many bereaved parents. It was painful for me. However, others feel joy and celebrate their child's birthday after they have passed. Everyone's resolve and approach to losing a child is an individual decision. It's best to be resilient in your choices to protect your mental health and allow healing to take place.

## FEELING GUILTY

It is a fact that loneliness and a heavy heart set in after the initial shock of losing a loved one. You believe the passion for your child will get you through; your child would not want you to be so sad for so long, but after the first two months, everything remained a challenge for me. Your loved one is constantly on your mind.

Spending time with my other daughter was helpful. Grieving together and engaging in lengthy discussions about our feelings was beneficial. She had crying episodes, feeling guilty about her last conversation with Amanda, letting her know she wasn't going to move to South Carolina. Unfortunately, that was the night she died. I struggled with guilt, too; perhaps if I had still been in South Carolina, I might have visited that day and could have saved her.

I visited my son. He seemed to be doing well. He wrote a letter expressing his feelings; there was some guilt and despair about Amanda. Siblings feel guilty when they think about what they could have done to change the outcome. There is no room for remorse, but these feelings arise in parents, siblings, and friends.

## TRYING TO MANAGE GRIEF

Grieving does not subside in the second month. As friends and family visit, it distracts you temporarily. It becomes challenging to stay strong and act normal. You have a difficult time believing your child is no longer with you.

This feeling may surprise some, but, in a way, you don't want the pain to go away because experiencing that pain shows your deep love for your child, and getting over it doesn't seem right. You want to believe there is light at the end of the tunnel, but in the second month, you may still feel the darkness.

A smile from my wife—it was Halloween night. I did not see my wife smile once during the month following Amanda's death. When the neighborhood children came to our door, my wife jumped up and went outside to pass out candy and greet the parents. There was joy in watching the children from inside as they approached the door. I saw my wife smiling; for a few moments, she was happy. It gave me a warm feeling. With all the grieving, I saw a glimmer of happiness in my wife, and it gave me hope that, one day, I would smile again, too. You pray to God that someday, the Grief will end, and you will experience happiness again.

My former wife, Amanda's mom, continued to go through a grueling time in South Carolina. While we grieved in Maryland, I wondered how she managed her Grief with the pressure of emptying Amanda's apartment, selling her car, gathering her clothes, and taking care of her cats. Amanda loved animals, and her cats were special to her. However, managing Grief when gathering personal items and picking up the pieces of your child's life is a grueling experience.

## GRIEVING ALONE

Reading books became a daily occurrence. There are five stages of Grief, but no actual sequential order to these stages. Everyone grieves differently. The early stage of Grief is denial. For me, it was shock and trauma. The latter stage of Grief is depression. I agree.

Because Amanda's death was so unexpected, the shock and trauma brought me to the brink of nonstop tears and uncontrolled shaking. A bereaved parent knows no pain is worse than first hearing that your child is gone. It's a stab in the heart.

After two months, the shaking would come and go, and the tears lessened, but the intense Grief, sadness, and emptiness

remained. I began to grieve more privately because most people feel that a man should not extend his Grief. Our culture sees
men as weak when they grieve too long.

### Reflection:

To expand on this thought, reading about our culture and la-
beling how men should handle tragedy is sad. If men get emotional, they are deemed weak. Stay strong, they say; be the rock
for your family. Some people may mention that you are lucky to
have other children and must be there for them. People have
good intentions, but I'm afraid I have to disagree that men are
weak if they grieve. It takes a lot of courage and strength to
weep. Cry, let it all out, because if you don't, you'll go crazy
holding it in. How could a bereaved parent ever get well if they
suppress the despair and pain? It's not possible.

# CHAPTER 11

# TRYING TO REGAIN STABILITY

TO BECOME MORE active, I ventured out to play tennis; it was the first time I had participated in an athletic activity in five weeks. My friends expressed their sorrow, but we avoided an extended conversation; I wanted to go out on the tennis court and not get emotional. It provided some relief to get some exercise.

When we finished playing, my friend sat with me and asked some questions. When you are in despair, you know the difficult challenge in your mind to stay calm when you discuss losing your child. So you silently pray that you won't become emotional to the point of a public meltdown.

He is a kind friend and generously donated to Ellie's "Go Fund Me" account, even though I'd only known him a few weeks. It felt good to have a new friend and feel comfortable opening up to him. But as I drove away, the floodgates opened, and I became emotionally overwhelmed. After five weeks, there were unanswered questions about what had happened. The long wait for answers seemed endless.

After 40-plus days, it continued to be challenging to wake up in the morning; you pray for the pain to lessen. You try to stay positive but avoiding the Grief is complicated.

Grief is like trying to hold 200 pounds above your head, but the weight becomes too much to bear, and it drops on you, crushing your spirit. I despised the pain. Getting over the pain is the pain. Even with all the blessings and family, the painful Grief penetrates your mind and body.

You push yourself to stay strong, get well, and believe that one day, you will be OK.

## Challenges being with family and friends

As friends and family visit, the challenges of seeing people most likely will exhaust your energy. Grief stays deep in your heart and drains your soul.

My mother- and father-in-law came to stay with us. They were in their early 90s and had been married for 70+ years. I engaged in several heart-to-heart talks with my father-in-law. It was emotional and challenging speaking about Amanda. The disbelief does not end. It gets redundant, but this is Grief; the unexpected emotions repeat daily. There are unending challenges every day, and you must accept that there will be exhausting times when the conversation should be enjoyable and is not.

## Stress in Marriage

As with many marriages, there will be minor disagreements along the way. Sometimes my wife and I would have small arguments. With so much company, there was a need to decompress and be alone. The pressure and stress were building in her, also.

She was upset with me for not appreciating anything she'd done: the house, our kids, our marriage. I knew she was right. But it did feel like nothing mattered to me; it was all about dealing with deep emotional pain and trying my best to survive the days.

You try to get through the sadness. I looked at my wife and said, "I am trying to be happy," but the tears came again, and I couldn't fake it. There was nothing she or anyone could do to help. She recommended professional help. I tended to agree but wasn't ready. Connecting with parents who also lost a child flooded my thoughts. There was a sincere need to communicate with people who had also lost a child.

### Reflection:

Over the first year, you don't realize it at the time, but birthdays, attending family events, and stress in your marriage or partnership ease. You begin accepting the unwelcome changes in your life and feel you can make it through. After a year, you will feel or begin to think that you can survive and live your life without your child. I never believed that this could happen early on after Amanda died. Of course, there will always be private moments with tears. But you will welcome these tears. I set time aside at precious personal moments throughout the year and didn't avoid the emotions moving forward. It is what bereaved parents do to survive.

# CHAPTER 12

# EXPECTATIONS OF GRIEF

## SHE IS REALLY GONE

It may be one of the worst days to remember when reality hits you. I finally said out loud, "Amanda is really gone!"

"She is really gone!" "She is really gone!" "Amanda is really gone!" Grieving for forty-five days, I still couldn't believe what happened was true.

You know in your mind that your child is gone, but your heart takes longer to accept your loss. The pain sporadically became less intense, my emotions were exhausted, and my anxiety seemed to ease. But then the sadness, intensity, and reality of never seeing Amanda again would return; it felt like a never-ending cycle.

**Reflection:**

A year later, you remember certain days of Grief. But as there are many days of despair, this was one day never to be forgotten. It is the day that you realize you will never see your child again. You see, the first 45 days, you are numb. You are in a world that has turned upside down. Your mind protects you from the trauma. As you come out of the shock and numbness, on this day, there is the unexplainable reality when you actually say the words that your child is really gone. There will be many instances of "No

Greater Pain" to your soul during this journey. It was another explicit day that stayed etched in my memory.

## UNEXPECTED AND NEVER PREPARED FOR THIS

When your child calls every day to say hello and ends with 'I love you,' then dies unexpectedly, nothing can prepare you for the emotional and physiological pain. It's not like a prolonged illness that you can prepare for; you can't prepare for the pain of losing a child, no matter how it happens. It is still hell. There is obvious joy when your child calls. I began to look forward to hearing from her and our video chats. I will always cherish the audio messages and videos of Amanda I saved. You can never prepare for the unexpected, and the anguish of your child's death is always with you.

## THE WAVES OF GRIEF

I read an analogy about Grief and how it relates to waves in an ocean. Losing a child feels like standing on the ocean shore when a big wave hits you and knocks you down. As you try to get up, another giant wave hits you and knocks you down, and another and another. You can't get up. Later, the huge waves come less frequently. You still can't get up, but at least the frequency of the waves slows down. Finally, the waves aren't as big; you can stand, but just barely. Just able to keep your balance, you are still unstable. The medium-sized waves keep hitting you, but you can stand, though still very weak. You hope the waves will become smaller and less frequent. Eventually, standing tall, you'll look out into the ocean and realize there can be a future without your child.

The waves will be significant for several months, and you will continue to fall. Then, as time passes, the Grief waves will become less frequent, and you can stand. But you stand alone, feeling empty and lonely.

You live and learn to manage it. There will always be waves; like the ocean, the waves never stop. All a bereaved parent can do is pray for strength, carry the burden, and keep balanced during the emotional rushes.

# CHAPTER 13

# THE CIRCLE OF EMOTIONS – FAMILY EVENTS

## ELLIE'S BIRTHDAY

Six weeks after my daughter died, we celebrated Ellie's third birthday in November.

My wife and I attended her party at her grandmother's house. Seeing her father, his mom, his stepdad, and all her church friends at their home was a warming feeling. Ellie was overwhelmed with joy—so many presents. She seemed to adjust to any home environment. Ellie loved her grandmother and showed affection toward her dad. It was bittersweet thinking what a great party it would have been with Amanda.

At their home, there was one picture of Amanda on the refrigerator mixed in with many other photos. The family was unsure if showing pictures of her mom at her birthday party would upset her. They needed to figure out how it would affect her, which was understandable. However, everyone had different thoughts on how to manage her loss.

When Ellie was at our home, I showed her pictures and videos of her mom, and she seemed happy to see them. It was a way to ensure that Ellie always remembered her mom.

I read that children 2-3 years old grieve and miss their mom's smell and contact. A 3-year-old child will cry and miss her mom and that special nurturing, especially at night when all the activity subsides. That night, Ellie cried hard at 3 am, and I was heartbroken to see and hear her crying. She must have realized that her mom was gone and was grieving as children do when a tragedy occurs. Of course we stayed up throughout the night to comfort her.

## THE DAY AFTER

The day after we celebrated Ellie's birthday, some things resonated with me when observing everybody at the party. It was festive, with about 20 people attending. I was surprised there was no time set aside to have a silent moment in Amanda's honor. It felt like she was being avoided. I should have mentioned something, paused the party, and prayed for Amanda. It was not my party or my house, but I regretted not saying a prayer for Amanda in front of the whole group. Throughout the evening, I discussed Amanda, and everyone realized what a good mom she had become. She spent considerable time teaching Ellie words, shapes, colors, and manners.

After Ellie's birthday, I spoke to my former wife's husband. He mentioned, his wife, Amanda's mom, had a panic attack and considered going to the hospital that night but decided to stay home. She had a difficult time breathing. In addition, she experienced painful weekends because Amanda spent most of her weekend time with her mom.

Amanda made several heartfelt cards expressing how she loved her. Her mom was her best friend, and she appreciated everything she did to make her life so happy and healthy.

## Trying to Move Forward

When grieving, it is essential to keep busy in a healthy way. So I tried to move forward with general activities.

You realize that it becomes challenging to get through the Grief alone. It was time to start searching for someone to talk to, hoping to find someone around my age who recently lost a child. It is common for a bereaved parent to search for someone who has been through this level of pain. There was a strong desire to find a counselor or medical professional who had also lost a child.

In the meantime, I grieved in my own personal way.

Thanksgiving was approaching, and so was Christmas. You think to yourself, *So soon!* You wish for more time to feel better before facing the holidays. You become fearful that people are going to expect too much. There wasn't a strong desire to visit our extended family because it would be stressful to appreciate everyone's joy while you were still in deep sorrow.

You begin to protect yourself, even if some family members may not understand. Fortunately, my family and friends all understood and showed considerable compassion.

## Missing your loved one - emptiness

Nighttime grieving is more intense than during the day, like a cold or a fever. Nights can be very lonely. You may spend most of the night awake, not crying but missing your loved one and wishing to see or hear them again. It's a strange thing. Sometimes you feel your child is still alive when you look at a picture and think they are still here. It sounds crazy, but then the realization hits that you can never take another photo of your child, bringing a sadness that is deep and permanent. After 53 days, it was still difficult to grasp that she was gone.

### *Reflection:*

It is not uncommon for a bereaved parent to continue to experience deep "longing" feelings that are difficult to put into words. It is normal to have these feelings of missing your child that reach depths only a bereaved parent experiences. However, it's essential to realize that these deep "yearning" feelings are typical in "prolonged Grief." This grieving isn't straightforward, and you accept it will be challenging to manage for months and possibly years beyond your expectations.

## Feeling Lost

My wife and I decided to go out to dinner—get away and get some fresh air. She was feeling lost. She mentioned that she was not only grieving losing Amanda but also grieving that she was losing me. She missed the person I used to be. She understood what we were all going through. She was lonely and started tearing up at the restaurant. I felt terrible because I did not include her enough in my Grief, and she loved Amanda too. I would go down to our basement each night to be alone and grieve. That was my outlet but rethinking how this affected her, I realized the need to communicate openly so we could support each other. Being sorry and expressing it is the best path to maintaining a solid marriage. My mind was spinning, and I wanted to return to normal. At least, that was how it felt at the time. Grief from a severe traumatic loss changes your personality. You can't remain the person you were after the shocking death of your child.

## Friends' Support

After we moved into a new neighborhood in Maryland, the Project Manager for the home builder stopped by to give us a gift for Ellie. It was an extraordinary gift, a fine jewelry angel. This kind gesture emotionally moved my wife because this gentleman was coordinating the construction of multiple houses, and he found the time to get this gift to us. You realize that there are special people who surround you. You learn to appreciate such kind acts. Other friends texted us to let us know that they were still thinking of us and praying for our family to gain the strength to get through our early days of Grief.

Friends are imperative when you are struggling with Grief. A special friend continued to check in with me to see if we needed anything. I accepted his invitation to dinner, even though I thought it would be draining. It was my first time out with someone other than my wife. It was a good evening, and we talked about many different things. I discussed the gravity and depth of sadness and told him what was on my mind. It led to me dropping tears at the restaurant. It was embarrassing for me. I talked about Amanda and how she always showed her love and appreciation to everyone; it just melted my heart.

**Reflection:**

A bereaved parent has a difficult time discussing their lost child. The subject is avoided due to people not wanting to have that difficult conversation. However, over time, the discussions become easier. The emotions may still consume you early on, but it gets better with time. Remembering these past times, it took me about six months to discuss my child while being able to control my emotions with friends and acquaintances who would ask about my family.

## QUESTIONING EVERYTHING

Every parent who loses a loved one will question the "what ifs?" It is a natural process when there is such a loss. I constantly questioned my move from South Carolina to Maryland. "What if I had not moved back to Maryland? Maybe I would have been there the night she died. She was alone. I usually drove up to see her in the afternoon and stayed until 7 pm. My mind was still processing everything. Always exhausted and tired, with no energy, a bereaved parent can't avoid these thoughts. We questioned if we had made the right decision to move from South Carolina to Maryland to be near family.

We enjoyed Amanda, who lived only 40 minutes away in South Carolina. When we first moved back, everything was terrific. We moved into a new  home, my son was doing well, and my other daughter was settling into an apartment. We visited our siblings, parents, and children and enjoyed the grandchildren. Then in

the blink of an eye, Amanda died, my son experienced some difficulties with the initial shock, and my other daughter relocated.
My wife's daughter and her husband moved from Maryland to
Pennsylvania, the health of my father-in-law and mother-in-law
was changing, my wife's brother became ill, and my wife's son
had foot surgery. Life can throw you a curveball in an instant.

We felt like a tornado hit us. But maybe God had his way of providing some strength and hope. My point is this: Life constantly
changes for everyone—some for the better and some for the
worse. So keeping positive and appreciating the simple things in
life is a good way forward. It helped me tremendously.

Many people came forward to support us with our Grief. My son
attended Grief counseling sessions and seemed much better.
My daughter landed a new job and received Grief counseling at
a Christian retreat. My stepdaughter and her husband resettled
in PA, and my other stepson successfully underwent surgery.

# CHAPTER 14

# HOLIDAY BE-WILDERNESS

## THE BIBLE

## STAYING BUSY

I gathered Amanda's Bible, and as I read through the pages, it was a bit surprising how much Amanda read every part of this Bible. She marked the Psalms for comfort, the miracles described in the New Testament by Mathew, Mark, John, and Luke, and she bookmarked Proverbs 31. In addition, she read one Proverb a day based on the day of the month. So I planned to read this Bible cover to cover to gain more knowledge. It was a good version of the Bible that described the meanings in terms for easier understanding. It was essential to begin doing something to help myself heal; this was a good start.

The Bible seemed to be most important to her. It was a goal of mine to try to understand God's ways and why life can be so cruel yet so rewarding in other ways.

## FEELING LIKE DAY 1 OVER AND OVER

As I approached 60 days, in my mind, as crazy as it may seem, I still could not accept that my daughter was gone. Too often, the Grief will hit you unexpectedly when you again realize that you will never see your loved one again. I know I am repeating this statement. It is a truthful occurrence during traumatic times. Acknowledging and accepting your child's death will always be difficult.

Based on the books I have read, a bereaved parent takes five to ten months to accept a child's death, and maybe much longer. My wife kept mentioning that she was also grieving Amanda's loss, which was extremely difficult. Suffering causes difficulties and stress; it becomes a mountain to climb to feel normal again. You feel helpless. I would read, write, and try to keep busy, but I would continue to shed tears at some point every day. Tears lessen the pain; they do. After a while, these episodes slowed down my heart and anxiety. If you have a spouse or significant other, their support is critical to getting well. My wife would hold me at night when my body started shaking, usually in the wee hours of the morning, and her support helped tremendously.

### Reflection:

Be prepared. For a grieving parent, your physical looks may change drastically. It's from the stress and heartbreak that you ex-perience. It is unavoidable. You will see how you have changed when you look in the mirror and can't believe what you see. This grieving takes a toll on you physically, possibly showing in your drained face, weight loss, sunken cheeks, and swollen eyes. Your smile will disappear. You realize that you must find the energy to stay strong and improve. Then you convince yourself to dig deep to manage your emotions so you can become a healthier version of yourself. Your loved one would not want to see you suffer, so you become more resilient to get through your tragedy and move forward. Over time, you will feel relief from the stress. I noticed improved changes in my physical appearance thirteen

months after my child died. It takes time to heal physically and
mentally.

## Emotional days continue

You realize that Grief makes you think about an abundance of
things, and everything becomes magnified. Yet I felt at peace,
believing that Amanda knew how much we all loved her through
our tears.

Reading so many books about Grief, you understand that it is normal to be emotional and fragile over weeks and months. Would
my Grief last a year? Two years? A bereaved parent doesn't know
where the end is because you realize that part of this Grief will
never end. You can't rush it; you have to live through it. After two
months, my Grief was not as debilitating as it was earlier, but I
still felt extreme mental pain and sadness.

A friend of mine lost his son several years ago. His son was walking downtown in a local city, was clubbed from behind for no
reason, and lost his life. My friend experienced the saddest of
times and had been through unimaginable Grief. After eight
years, he still has days of suffering and has said that his late son
is always on his mind. He started a foundation in honor of his
son and involved himself in speaking engagements to discuss his
loss and journey through Grief. He decided to avoid individual
and group counseling. Instead, he grieved with his wife more
privately, and they each had their way of grieving the loss of their
son. He mentioned that the memories and loss of his son were in
his soul permanently, and he would always have that feeling of
significant loss, now and forever. After almost two months since

Amanda died, I understood how he felt and expected this same hardship in the future.

## Day before Thanksgiving

A bereaved mother or father will have many flashbacks about their loved one. You carry yourself through life with your child's heart on your shoulder. On this particular day, I was in the grocery store buying food for Thanksgiving. I remembered the previous year, when I brought turkey, stuffing, potatoes, and green bean casserole to Amanda; she loved it. It was a memory that was unforgettable. She was excited and looking forward to spending Thanksgiving with me the year she died. Someday, as a bereaved parent, you will reflect on specific events and remember the joyful memories, not the sadness they may bring you.

Being thankful when your child is gone on Thanksgiving is a challenge. The seat at the table is empty. A bereaved parent wants to trade places with their deceased loved one so they can live a long, happy life. I visited Amanda's gravesite that evening. Looking down at her grave, I knew she was just four feet away. It was excruciating to think she was underground and only four feet away, and I couldn't get her out, save her, hold her, or talk to her one more time. You wonder why God took your precious child away.

## The Coroners' Toxicology Report is in

Two months after my daughter's death, I received a text message from my former wife mid-week, at 4:02 pm. She mentioned that the coroner called her with the toxicology report. She did not ask for the results immediately because she wanted to prepare herself and get through the holiday. My former wife decided to wait and call him back on Monday, November 30, to discuss the results. Ironically, this was Amanda's birthdate. I would wait also. Thanksgiving was one day away, and we would have family over for dinner. It was stressful; waiting for the report resulted in high anxiety, not quite leading to an anxiety attack, but close to it. My heart started pounding, and the shaking began. It turned out to be a difficult, emotional day. A bereaved parent becomes fearful of the truth.

## THANKSGIVING DAY

Of course, a bereaved parent feels sadness on Thanksgiving Day. My family visited on this holiday, which turned out to be a busy day. You know it will be an exhausting day but try to put on a solid front. You experience those longing thoughts of missing your child. It takes an enormous amount of energy to hold Grief inside. The toxicology report was on my mind, but I attempted to exclude these thoughts for the day. The day was beautiful and heartwarming in many ways. It was nice having a family gathering over for dinner.

It was 8 pm, and the dinner gathering was heartwarming, with good food. My wife and I made most of the dinner spread over two days, keeping us busy. My children and the grandkids were a welcome sight, and it was good to have some activity in the house. My son and his wife were doing well. The children were active, and it was an enjoyable day. The children had a blast, and it was good to see my son and his wife. They helped out a lot with the dinner activities and cleaning the kitchen. There was not much discussion about Amanda except for prayer at dinner, because it was just a day to try to enjoy Thanksgiving and not get everyone sad.

**Reflection:**

One year later, I can state that you will feel you are going through the motions with hollowness and emptiness. So you grasp and hold onto simple memories to feel some joy. Being with a compassionate family was a memory that stayed with me. It is normal to feel lost and sad inside during holidays, but you remember the joyful occasions with family. Unfortunately, there will be many more holidays to endure without your child. The longing and yearning for your child during family gatherings become an unavoidable heartache. But I am here to tell you that you will eventually look forward to these times. It may take one or two years, but you realize your child would want you to enjoy the holidays and not cave into the weight of Grief.

## DAY AFTER THANKSGIVING

I was determined to call the coroner the day after Thanksgiving. The toxicology report was in, and my former wife gave me the contact information. I needed to know the results and was up most of the night, filled with anxiety about this call. So I decided to make the call and have tissues ready, no matter the outcome.

It was 9:30 am on a Friday. I called the coroner four times with no answer. He wasn't available. Maybe I wasn't ready to hear the results. After a holiday, as joyous as it may have been, you are exhausted. The wave of Grief has a mind of its own. You feel it will never end. I fell asleep in the recliner for three hours that afternoon and woke up in the dark. Sometimes it is best to grieve alone, and with more holidays approaching, everybody would be coming to visit for Christmas. It becomes a lot to bear, even though you know everyone is caring and compassionate. You become lonely in Grief after all the other emotions you experience. It is a deep pain, and challenging to explain; it feels bottomless, and you don't know how to end it.

## SEARCHING FOR THE ANSWER

It was a Saturday morning. My wife was angry with me, probably because of something I had said. I was unsure what that was, but I only wanted her to understand that being around family and friends was difficult. A bereaved parent understands the depth of emotions.

Despite developing Plantar Fasciitis in my foot, I decided to play tennis a few days after Thanksgiving. It seemed that physically, the Grief was taking its toll. I decided to call the coroner again after playing tennis. There was hesitation because anxiety builds up fast when you fear the answers. I thought, *He may answer the phone today.* I was concerned about his results, and it was difficult even to make the call. If he did not answer, I figured it would be Monday or Tuesday when Amanda's mom called him. So I called on Saturday, and yet again, there was no answer. It was a weekend, and the coroner must have taken the weekend off. Waiting for answers on autopsy results is something you wish on nobody. I kept seeing visions of Amanda lying on the floor, collapsed in front of the TV, with little Ellie trying to wake her up. It was an excruciating thought, and I wondered if Ellie had seen her fall to the floor while watching TV. She may be able to remember or tell me when she is a little older.

# CHAPTER 15

# THE TOXICOLOGY REPORT

## THOUGHTS OF EMPTINESS

Grief makes you feel like you are in the Twilight Zone, not feeling, not crying, not thinking, and not looking forward to the day in front of you. Any loss is a life-changing event, but nothing compares to losing a child. It is not the correct order of things. Figuring out a world without your loved one feels lonely and sad. You try to figure out what to do every day. You ask yourself, "What do I want out of life? How can I ever be happy again?" You are in a confused state of mind. You try to find peace, happiness, and a small piece of joy once a day. I felt blessed to have my family and grandchildren. In Grief or complicated Grief, the pain of your loss supersedes everything. You know you have to manage the Grief to heal. It was going to be a long journey, and I hoped there would not be excessive long-term anguish along the way.

## THE REPORT IS RECEIVED

The weekend passed, and it was 9:30 am Monday when I received a text message from Amanda's mom. She finally talked to the coroner and wanted me to call her. I showed the text to my wife and decided to drive to the cemetery alone to call her. It felt like an emotional tsunami was approaching, and I feared what I might learn about how Amanda died. There would be no good news about this. It didn't matter how Amanda died in the end, but I still wanted to know. I hoped she did not suffer. So I finally received an answer. My former wife gave me the news.

The coroner ruled Amanda's death as an accidental overdose of the anti-depressant drug Prozac. Her blood level showed a fatal serotonin level in her system. It was also possible that the pre-scribed medicine was a deadly mix. Her doctor had prescribed Trazadone for sleep and Intuniv, an ADHD medication, for anxi-ety. This mix may have had a catastrophic adverse effect and dropped Amanda's blood pressure to dangerously low levels. Amanda's heart stopped. She fell to the floor. Doctors advised us that the mix of medicines could have led to a heart episode with insufficient blood pressure for the heart to restart. It was heartbreaking and so difficult to understand.

The day Amanda died was the most emotional, debilitating day for all of us. So many things go through your mind when a trag-edy like this occurs. I knew that this day would also be most difficult, no matter what the coroner told us. Returning home, I collapsed on the couch in disbelief. This day ended, and the night would be a sleepless one.

A bereaved parent wonders about coincidences. It was astonish-ing to me that we found out the cause of Amanda's death on her birthday, November 30.

### Reflection:

As the months pass by during the first and second year, a be-reaved parent should not become consumed by not having all the answers. I learned this the hard way. Bereaved parents want to understand everything about their child's death; sometimes, that is impossible. You can become consumed thinking about your loved one's state of mind on that last day. I wondered if my daughter experienced pain at the very end. But you learn to avoid the negative thoughts and realize that you will never survive the heartache if you stay overwhelmed with all the details you cannot understand. I learned to avoid these thoughts and focused on all the delightful memories.

# CHAPTER 16

# AMANDA'S BIRTHDAY

AMANDA WOULD HAVE been 35 years old on this day. Therefore, I will share the letter I wrote to her on her birthday.

As a bereaved parent, your mind focuses on what you could or should have done better as a mother or father. When you grieve, you think about all the support you provided for your child. There is a guilt that confronts you when you grieve, and sometimes you become overwhelmed by what you could have done during your loved one's lifetime to provide better support. Everyone has regrets. It is unavoidable. Then you realize all the good things you did to help your child from early adulthood. There was no need to address all the good memories. Amanda knew I supported her; that is why we built such a loving father-daughter relationship.

# Letter to Amanda on her birthday

**From Dad,**

It's your birthday, and it's not a happy one for me. It's my first birthday without you, and I still can't believe this has happened. Our whole family has always loved you. You are precious to me, your mom, your brothers, your sisters, and your step-parents. There are many reasons why you have been so special. But, of course, one of my happiest moments was when you were born, and raising you in the early years was easy because you were so affectionate and always happy.

It goes back to when I saw your face light up when you were six years old and were excited to go to school. I will always cherish this photo. You were always so appreciative and so thankful, even at that age.

Now we are bereaved parents. There is guilt in believing we could have done more to care for you more often in your adult years. You had some anxiety issues, and we regret not helping you more. I didn't realize that you had difficult times. You protected us by not telling us about your struggles. If we had only known... It's painful to think of your struggles through the years. You were so independent and took on life's ups and downs amazingly with your great attitude.

You refrained from telling us your problems because you loved us so much and did not want to cause any stress in our lives. You were always thinking of other people and tried to protect us from stress by bearing some difficulties in private. Our whole family loves you, Amanda, and we will love you forever.

You always gave everything possible to less fortunate people. It didn't matter if you only had five dollars in your pocket; you always helped out a stranger or friend. But on the other hand, you worried about us too much. It was heartbreaking to me that you dealt with severe anxiety issues. Today, your mother and I would trade places with you in a minute.

You never talked back to me and were never disrespectful. Even when there were "tough love" moments, you just listened and were sorry for whatever you may have done. You loved us so much that it didn't matter during those instances of a father's tough love. You always were kind and respectful. I don't remember you raising your voice to your mom or me. You always respected the family. Throughout all the years, you never directed any anger or disrespect toward us. We will cherish that love and affection you showed for the rest of our lives.

We enjoyed good, loving times, and you blossomed into a responsible, loving mother. I enjoyed visiting you often and spending time with you and Ellie. You appreciated everything, and your mom made much of this possible. Ellie changed your life, and I don't know why God took your life away. I know you had strong faith. I read all your notes and looked through the Bible you read. Your strong faith was impressive to me.

On your 35th birthday, we will carry sadness in our hearts. I know you don't want us to feel this way, but it should show you the deep love the whole family still has for you. We miss you dearly, Amanda, and we hope to see you in heaven.

Someday, I hope you will send me a sign to let us know you are safe and happy. Eventually, I will wake up with contentment and fulfillment after seeing and talking to you in a dream. You can somehow show me your spirit is alive and well.

We all love you, Amanda! Rest peacefully. We will all take care of Ellie. I am sure that you miss her. I know that she misses you. We will ensure that she always remembers you and show her your love through your pictures and videos. I pray you can look down on us to see how we are now living our lives, taking care of Ellie, and never forgetting you in our memories.

**Love, Dad**

*Reflection:*

A typical method counselors recommend to those who have lost a loved one is to write a letter expressing all those feelings and thoughts that flood your mind. Starting a daily journal can re-direct your heartbreak to a better place. Writing it down may sound childish and silly, but it does help to flush out all those feelings and express your love for your child. There are always some regrets in one's life, and we are all human, none without sin. Writing this letter was therapeutic. Revisiting your past writings will help you remember the healing journey.

# CHAPTER 17

# EMOTIONAL ROLLERCOASTERS

## PHYSICAL AND EMOTIONAL PAIN

During my third month after Amanda died, my level of emotion started changing for the better. There would still be tears, especially on Amanda's birthday and the quiet day after. Amanda was always in my thoughts every minute of the day. My body didn't shake as hard, and the tears lasted for about 20 minutes. It was better than shedding tears for hours, but the exhaustion continued. I could sleep any time of the day and usually went to bed around 8 pm and read for a while, somewhat numb and unfocused. After two-plus months, the emptiness remained deep.

The physical pain and anguish lessen, but the sadness stays with you. You hope tomorrow will be a better day. One step at a time is OK, and you realize there will be setbacks. The days seemed to repeat themselves.

You try to stay busy, work on small projects, and attempt to be more active, but the reality is that you go through the motions, feeling empty. The thought of never seeing your child again is debilitating. You live a nightmare every day, and it is challenging for a bereaved parent to accept this reality.

## Imagine Heaven

I read another book titled *Imagine Heaven*. It's a book about people who have died for a short time and saw heaven or what they think was heaven. They have come back to life out of comas, accidents, and deadly sicknesses and have lived to tell about the life they saw after death. But it was more than that. These were people who flat-lined, with no brain activity, no heartbeat, and were presumed dead. There are thousands of people who describe their stories. The author selected 100 people who had nothing to gain financially. They were doctors, nurses, lawyers, and honest people who lived through this experience that brought them to God. It gave me hope. I prayed and hoped to see Amanda and my parents again someday. This book ties the Bible into the actual reported events. Thousands of people have died and come back to share their afterlife experiences.

I learned about the miracles that occurred, and it was beginning to restore some of my broken faith. Nevertheless, I ended my days thinking about the Afterlife. It was incomprehensible to believe that one lives in darkness after death.

## Expressions of Grief

Grief is painful both mentally and physically. You must endure and embrace it in a certain way because the more you have loved, the more profound and painful the Grief. It shows that love has far-reaching bounds. It was healing for me to grieve and shed tears. Feeling empty is part of Grief. God gives us the experiences of loving, losing, happiness, and sadness. It means that we are alive and well in many ways. At least we live our lives capturing every emotion possible. You become more sensitive to people's feelings and reactions. You begin to reach out and try to connect with current friends, family, and new friends and neighbors. Grief makes you want to be more compassionate and caring than ever before. However, this attitude doesn't include everyone. Sometimes you have to move away from people who seem uncaring and non-responsive to your loss.

### Reflection:

After a year has passed, you may notice that not everyone has the same outlook on life, and sometimes it is wise to stay away from stressful situations and people you don't feel are real. Actions usually speak louder than words. Some people avoid you during a crisis, and some compassionate and caring people step forward and express their sympathies. But remember that many people want to give you space, which is a kindhearted approach. Not everyone knows how to react to a grieving parent, which is understandable. We are all human beings who are not perfect, and we all make mistakes in life. Forgive and don't judge; it is the best way forward.

# CHAPTER 18

# UNEXPECTED EMOTIONS

## NEW WAVES OF UNEXPECTED GRIEF

Seventy days since Amanda's passing seemed like a long time, but it wasn't.

Waking up for the day continued to be a challenge. First, you think of your child; the trauma of being shocked by their death pushes your emotions out of control. Next, your body continues to shake at night while falling asleep. Then you stare out the window for the longest time and have no thoughts.

You have a blank mind feeling, like you are in a fog. The fogginess results from your mind protecting you from traumatic thoughts, just as people can't recall moments before a bad car accident.

You begin to wonder if you will die at a scheduled time. You ask yourself questions. "Why did my daughter die at age 34 while I am still alive? Why haven't I died? Has God kept me healthy to serve a purpose on this earth? Why am I still here, and my daughter is gone?"

It didn't make sense to me. Yet I needed to trust in God and pray that I would see my daughter again.

Consider this: Psalm 139:16 clearly states in the Bible that our daily life is measured. God knows the exact time we will die.

He knows when He's going to call us home. Therefore, you can do nothing to extend your life span (or someone else's) by one-tenth of a second.

## Bearing the Unbearable

I finished reading another book titled *Bearing the Unbearable*. These books were beneficial for me in some ways, but it becomes emotional when you read about the same types of anguish. They do offer perspectives on how parents deal with losing a child. Reading helps, and so does writing. So I decided to write this book. I put my thoughts on paper to survive each day.

You realize early on that this loss is unbearable and that getting past the suffering will take a significant amount of time. Once you get past the anguish, you have the pain and loneliness that stays with you for a long time. There are ways to shed the loneliness by seeking help through counseling, taking better care of yourself, and engaging in some activities to help you feel more comfortable. It is a reality you have to accept. Once you accept it, continuing with your life is a little bit easier.

**Reflection:**

There is much to realize about the notion that crying proves love for your child. These emotions are expertly discussed in the book, "Bearing the Unbearable." You genuinely feel your child is looking down on you and realizes how much love is in your heart. Referring to the book I read, *Imagine Heaven*, I believed joy filled her in God's bright light. So many people have experienced Near Death Experiences, and the consistency of these stories is remarkable. More than profound, these stories line up with many scriptures in the Bible; it makes you believe in God to the fullest extent of your being.

## RESISTING ACCEPTING MY LOSS

As I reflected on how Grief affects you, one thing that stood out was the resistance to accept and believe that your loved one is no longer here. It didn't seem permanent or final.

Since Amanda's death, my wife has met and realized how many parents have lost a child or loved one. There are so many of us. So many people carry Grief and have lost so much. There are many horrible stories of parents losing their children in sad ways.

Joel Osteen, the well-known preacher of God, mentioned in a sermon that when a close family member dies, you have to accept it, move past it and forget about it if you are to move forward. He received significant backlash from many of his followers, and thousands of people responded by disputing these statements. You can never get over it and move on. You live with it. It becomes a part of you, and you carry forward that loss and learn how to manage it.

It was surprising to hear this from Joel Osteen. He is a sincere speaker, but when it comes to Grief, he might have been off base and incorrect in his message. Everyone has a different opinion about Grief, and there may be no right or wrong answers.

## ELLIE PROVIDES MORE JOY

When my granddaughter, Ellie, visited, the timing was perfect as I enjoyed her during the holidays. I saw happiness and joy.

Experiencing the joy of Ellie was vital to get through my Grief. When you grieve, you search for any relief. Ellie was so lovable. It was just what I needed. She reminded me of my daughter Amanda in so many ways. A bereaved parent has to learn to live with the sadness and look to the future to find some joy. Ellie provided that joy.

My daughter's death affected everyone's life, especially Ellie's. She always wanted a "mommy" kiss at bedtime. She missed her mom and would start tearing up. It was heartbreaking. You don't know what is in a three-year-old's mind, but you know that a little girl will miss her mom's comfort and loving affection.

## GRIEF AND SELF PRESERVATION

You ask yourself, how long is too long to grieve? After 90 days of extreme Grief, each person who owns their Grief understands there is no time limit. You realize that grieving is not only healthy but is necessary to get through the most intense pain a human being can endure. So you learn to manage your Grief and protect yourself when suffering becomes overwhelming. Looking at pictures of my lost daughter and listening to voicemail messages was emotional. Sometimes you have to give yourself a break and do other things to keep your mind occupied for a short while. When I listened to the voicemails shortly after the funeral, the emotion devastated me, and I could barely breathe. So you resist those circumstances to give your feelings a break.

Additional reading about Grief resulted in an improved state of mind. I realized it was OK to get emotional, be sad, and grieve every day if that was how I felt.

Spending time alone to reflect on the memories is healthy. You learn that it's essential not to let it overwhelm you to the point that you cannot function throughout the day. Research studies show that tears have a healthy chemical released during traumatic times. You feel better or relieved after a good cry.

### Reflection:

Remember, for every loss, there is someone out there who has experienced even more tragedy than can be imagined. Life as we know it changes us with the tragedies we face. Many people get up and live with joy and normalcy after a personal loss. It takes time, and you have to embrace these challenges. There is always some hope, and you must have hope to be happy again. It's the only way forward. Yes, you revisit your emotions and manage them differently after a year. You do learn to protect yourself when suffering becomes overwhelming. Find joy in any way you can. Sometimes joy and happiness come in small pieces, but eventually, those pieces begin to merge, and you begin to realize that you will make it.

# CHAPTER 19

# SADNESS AROUND CHRISTMAS

## TELLING MY CHILDREN ABOUT AMANDA'S DEATH

I invited my son to our home to tell him how Amanda died. We received details in the toxicology report, and it was time to sit down and provide the necessary information. As I mentioned, Amanda's toxicology report indicated that her death was an accidental overdose of Prozac and a possible fatal mix of prescription medicine that caused her death.

Amanda had a lot of anxiety and some sadness for various reasons. Her panic attacks resulted from worrying, and Prozac helped her stay calm.

My son was doing very well. I gave him the news. He was way ahead of me regarding how to handle Grief. It showed through his logic and rationale. I told my other children the results by phone.

## ENDLESS GRIEF

It's undeniable that it gets more difficult during the holidays. You brace for it, manage the days, and can't hold it any longer. Then the floodgates open up, and you fall apart in Grief in a private moment. It is something you expect, but you try your best to endure the physical and emotional pain that comes with it.

During holidays, you miss your loved one so much that it physically hurts. But the reality is that your child is never coming back, and it is finally starting to set in. You realize that you are never going to see your child again. You are never going to hear their voice again. You don't want to admit to yourself that they are gone. Yet you still feel their presence.

You lie down at night before sleeping and pray for a dream. It doesn't come, and you wake up disappointed because you didn't get to see or talk to your child in a dream. You are longing for anything to help you stay close and remember. You lie there, willing your child — no, begging your child — to come to see you.

You whisper in the darkness and ask God to let your child visit you in your dreams, and many dreamless nights follow. Unfortunately, it doesn't always work as you pray it would.

Yet you are always thinking of your loved one. When the sky is gray, and a patch of light finds its way through the clouds, you look for a heart. When you go shopping, you think about the last time you went shopping with your child.

You start seeing your child in other people. You think of your child when you laugh or cry because you will never forget those happy and sad times. When you post something on social media, you wait for their comment but realize it won't ever happen again.

You have random flashbacks, and you cherish those moments. People never say it, but they act as if grieving is something you eventually get over. That is the farthest thing from the truth, because Grief is endless; you will endure it for the love of your lost child.

When you lose someone you love, someone important to you, you don't think you will ever stop grieving. It just eventually becomes something you learn to cope with every day. You know that it's something you should stop doing, but you never do.

There's nothing wrong with missing someone who is gone. However, knowing and accepting that your child is never coming back will not make the pain of missing them any easier.

There is no right or wrong way to grieve someone's passing. Instead, it's learning to live with a chunk of yourself missing and filling that void the best way you can to make it through the tough times. You have to do what you can to make it through each day.

### Reflection:

Fourteen months after my daughter's death, the second time experiencing the holidays was less painful. Instead of hibernating in mental anguish and being overcome with sadness and emotion, I cautiously looked forward to being with family and grandchildren. You reach for joy. You pray that you can move forward with a new life without your child. I always felt my daughter's presence with me. You carry the memory of your child everywhere you go. So in the second year, the holidays, birthdays, and anniversaries were not as difficult for me as the first year. Everyone is different. I believe the hard work one puts in to heal and get past the acute and extended Grief will benefit all bereaved parents, even if you don't think so early on in this journey.

# CHAPTER 20

## THE THIRD MONTH

YOU REALIZE THAT life goes on, but those excruciating times crop up when you least expect it. During my journey, I noticed that the physical pain was not as excessive, but the sadness remained. New waves of emotions come unexpectedly, and Grief's effects take a toll on you. It is all about trying to bear the unbearable. In a way, the human mind protects you and resists accepting your loss.

You don't want to address the finality of your loss. But in the back of your mind, it is reality. As this nightmare of loss is all-consuming, you must consider self-preservation and taking care of yourself. So you look for joy. My granddaughter, Ellie, provided that joy. Grief has many emotional and physical effects; the days pass quickly, and others stand still. You learn and persevere in your challenges to get well.

### HITTING ROCK BOTTOM BEYOND 90 DAYS

As you try to move forward, you know that nothing has prepared you to live without your loved one. You are now a changed person. Your world is upended.

However, I can tell you that the pain does lessen over time, and you become open to getting well. You begin to care more deeply. It is normal to feel that you could have done something to help prevent this, and you question everything. But you will begin to move forward and start thinking of positive things, happy times, and good memories about your loved one. It gets better. I would have never believed that I could get better, but I did.

# DAY 100 - STORY - ACTS OF KINDNESS BRINGS TEARS

It was over 100 days since my daughter died, and I believed I was on the right track to surviving and healing, but this story brought me to tears and led to an emotional or mental meltdown. You try to be strong, but there are times that the Grief comes back and overtakes you at a moment's notice. Here is my story.

I cared for my granddaughter Ellie, Amanda's daughter, for eight days. She provided joy and love during this difficult time. I drove her back to South Carolina to drop her off with my former wife, who had acquired legal guardianship of Ellie. There was a bad snowstorm the night before this trip. There was no snow at my home north of the storm. I thought that the roads were clear.

I drove for an hour and saw signs that drivers should avoid the Interstate and take alternate routes. Finally, I reluctantly entered the Interstate because there was no snow evident. Fifteen minutes later, the traffic came to a standstill. There was a foot of snow and ice covering the trees.

The Virginia Department of Transportation (VDOT) closed the Interstate and the alternate routes south.

I was utterly stuck in traffic and didn't move for an hour. Then, finally, I exited on an alternate route; even secondary roads were barely open. I was genuinely concerned about being in the car with Ellie, my three-year-old granddaughter.

As I made my way, there were abandoned cars and trucks everywhere. Six inches of ice were on the trees, and many downed trees were blocking road access. The weight of ice snapped the power lines. Traffic on the secondary roads was nearly impassable. My anxiety felt uncontrollable, but I tried to remain calm as Ellie played and sang and told me to look at the pretty snow and ice on the trees. It was her first look at the snow, so she took it all in as I tried to be safe in the car. I moved slowly on the roads with minimal movement for two more hours.

There was no place to reverse as cars lined up behind me. Turning around on the road was impossible because they were narrow and covered in four inches of road ice. Cars were sliding off the road in front of me. A stalled tractor-trailer blocked the right side of the road. There was a narrow opening to pass, but cars alternated from the oncoming traffic in front of me. Finally, a car tried to pass and slid off the road right in front of me. At this point, I realized there was no safe way out, but after being in the car for five hours now, fortunately, there was enough gas to keep the heat on and be warm for Ellie. But it was a dire situation.

So I prayed that I could get through without sliding into the ditch. Cars behind me were honking their horn to move. So I started moving through the narrow passageway and realized a hill was farther ahead. I wanted to make it up the incline. As I proceeded forward, I slid sideways on the rear wheels, kept moving slowly, and made it through, just missing the other car that slid off the road in front of me. I barely made it up the hill. Meanwhile, little Ellie was singing Christmas songs and was unaware of the situation.

I called my wife, and she directed me to a route to a hotel a mile away. When I arrived at the hotel, it was a relief to make it somewhere safe and warm. After six hours in the car, I entered the hotel and observed about 100 people waiting to reserve a room in the lobby. It turned out that the Amtrak train stopped and unloaded all the passengers because a tree fell onto the track and it was impassable. So here I was in a hotel with 100 people. I approached the front counter and asked for a room. The hotel receptionist advised that no rooms were available and 38 people were on a waiting list. It was demoralizing. We didn't have a place to stay, and no hotels were nearby. It was impossible to go out to find another hotel. I sat in the lobby waiting for the Interstate to reopen. Exhausted and upset with worry, I wondered what I was going to do. Finally, the best thing to do was to sleep in the lobby if the Interstate did not reopen.

Then a lady approached me and asked if we were all right. I told her we were doing OK but I didn't know what to do. The kind lady offered Ellie a snack and was very nice. I felt a few tears dropping from my eyes because that was such a nice gesture. I was emotionally exhausted. She must have noticed my despair because 30 minutes later, she approached me and kindly offered me her room if she could get back on the train once they cleared the tree. The tree blocked the train from the night before. This lady's kind offer brought on more tears. Small friendly gestures are magnified when you are grieving. The lady who offered me her room spent the previous night sleeping in the car. It is amazing how kind some people can be.

Another hour passed, and I approached the front desk and asked again about any possibility of getting a room. The lady at the service desk mentioned that no rooms were available because they had booked them the previous night. She added my name to the waiting list.

Another gentleman approached me and must have seen my dilemma. He mentioned that his brother had reserved two rooms separately and he would offer his room and stay with his brother. His generous offer was, again, an unbelievable act of kindness. I was so appreciative and thanked him. Then, hoping for a cancellation, I mentioned being on the waiting list and said I wanted to see if a room would become available.

I knew that getting a room was doubtful. Another hour passed when the kind lady at the reservation desk motioned me to come forward. She said, "Give me your ID and credit card, and I will see what I can do." She subtly put her finger up her mouth and signaled quietly. She bumped me up to the top of the list. This gesture was an unbelievable act of kindness. Unfortunately, my emotions were uncontrollable, and I started to melt down.

She was so concerned, and she asked why I was so upset. I apologized and mentioned that my daughter passed away recently, and I was grieving.

Here I believed that I was doing OK because having Ellie for a week kept me busy, but the exhaustion and Grief were unavoidable. Then, after we sat in the lobby for another hour, she called me back up to the reception desk. She said there was one cancellation and told me that housekeeping had advised her that the room was ready for occupancy.

Looking at me with compassion, she mentioned that she had lost her husband and understood my Grief. She booked me the room from the one cancellation she received. She reduced the nightly rate significantly and offered me two complimentary breakfasts. I was overwhelmed with gratitude, not able to control the tears. As I turned around, all the people in the lobby looked at me with compassion, and all I could do was apologize for my emotions.

Her name was Lisa. She looked me in the eyes with a piercing and compassionate gaze and mentioned that she knew Grief. She noted that it had been three years since her husband died. I asked her, "When did the Grief end for you?" She calmly said, "Ron, the Grief never ends, but it will become more tolerable. The suffering will lessen over time, but it may never go away. So it's essential to stay strong and move forward with positive thoughts for your daughter. Be strong," she said as she gave me the keys to the room.

There were 850 car accidents that day, and the storm resulted in over 1000 stranded cars on the Interstate and the secondary roads. People slept in their vehicles. The streets opened far into the night. Yet God was with me that night and helped me realize that there is hope and faith, and you are not alone during Grief. God stood by me this day when life got overwhelming and desperate.

So I asked myself, did I have an emotional meltdown or breakdown? The answer was obvious. I'm not proud of this, but it's my truth.

## My emotional breakdown

As I checked out of the hotel the following day, Lisa was at the front desk. She worked the previous day late into the night and was there early in the morning. Lisa may have never left the hotel to go back to her home. As I checked out, I told her she was most generous and kind.

It was a time to work through this Grief and be more resilient. I intended to move forward with more strength because crying became my medical concern. This emotional episode may have been my "bottom" to Grief; all I could hope for was to keep trying to heal.

The Webster's dictionary definition of "Emotional breakdown":

"Emotional breakdown" is a term used to describe someone suffering from depression, anxiety, and acute stress disorder. An emotional breakdown means someone is experiencing insomnia and possibly emotional outbursts, including sadness – sometimes with an apparent cause – Shattered nerves and burnout – Emotional collapse, and nervous exhaustion.

Secondly, emotional breakdown describes a personal meltdown of an individual who doesn't know how to cope with present circumstances. These instances can include episodes of uncontrollable weeping, withdrawal from loved ones, and an inability to connect with everyday life.

Crying can be considered an emotional or mental breakdown. Unable to control tears — an overwhelmed feeling to concentrate or make decisions. Becoming moody — feeling low or depressed; feeling burnt out; emotional outbursts of uncontrollable fear, helplessness, or crying. A feeling of hopelessness.

### Reflection:

Reflecting on the previous year, I realized that most parents have their breaking points. Yes, I experienced many emotional meltdowns, too many to count. Your child dying is the breaking point of any human being with a heart. So when my child died, I couldn't suppress my emotions. Looking back at the million tears shed over the first year, I believe it took strength to let the emotions flow. Yes, you feel weak, vulnerable, helpless, and highly embarrassed. But you will learn to walk with pride with memories of your loved one. You have owned the Grief and will realize that not suppressing the emotions helped you heal.

# CHAPTER 21

# HOPE AND FAITH

## Signs from your lost child

There is one more story about my stay at the hotel that evening, following the nightmare of driving through a snowstorm. I will share one more hope of faith. It's all about signs from your loved one.

After we checked into the hotel room, it was time for little Ellie and me to turn in and sleep.

The Interstate was still closed for snow and ice clearing. I was exhausted. As we turned in, I placed Ellie on one side of the king bed, and I slept on the other side with my back toward Ellie. Two hours into the night, Ellie migrated over to me with my back to her, and she snuggled into me, placed her arm around my waist, and said, "Grandpa." I turned and said, "Are you awake, Ellie?" No response, Ellie was sound asleep, so I got up and positioned her back on the other side of the bed. Then an hour later, the same thing happened. Ellie slid over to my back, snuggled up, put her arm around my waist, and said, "Grandpa." I noticed that Ellie's eyes were closed and she was sound asleep.

Then my thoughts turned to my daughter Amanda, and I wondered silently if this was Amanda trying to comfort me from heaven. It seems ridiculous, but when you grieve, your mind wishes for signs from your loved one.

So I placed Ellie on the other side of the bed for the third time. An hour later, Ellie was again snuggled into my back with her arm over my waist, and she said, "Grandpa." At this moment, my tears started to flow silently. Ellie was sound asleep and still said, "Grandpa." I could not believe it. I placed Ellie on the other side of the bed for the fourth time and put a pillow between us because I needed some sleep. It was now three in the morning. Two hours later, with my back to Ellie, I felt Ellie again; she must have crawled over the pillow. She was sound asleep. My emotions flowed, and I believed at the time that this was Amanda giving me a sign that she was there with me, giving me some comfort. It sounds crazy, but believing in things that protect your mind during high emotional times is expected.

**Reflection:**

Over the first year and beyond, bereaved parents will be very aware of signs from their loved ones. Potential signs are described later in this book. You feel your child's presence in many ways. Your mind changes, and you emotionally strive for anything to survive the longing and despair of losing your child. There are many signs that you may see. They will come, and they will be personal only to you. So if and when they arrive, embrace them. Believe that your child is in heaven looking upon you and believe there is an afterlife and that you will someday see your child again.

## DEEP THOUGHTS OF MY GRIEF

A few days passed.

I was sitting alone thinking about my emotional meltdown just four days ago. During the fourth month, the internal pain remains; it stays with you for a long time. The pattern of waking up in the middle of the night with your mind racing feeds the anxiety. So I would breathe deeply and let my breath out slowly to calm down. These types of breathing techniques are helpful to slow the heart rate and relax. It becomes problematic when you reflect on the details of what happened.

Thinking ahead becomes difficult because you are still trying to survive each day. You don't want to admit that this is the final chapter. It's too soon to think that all this is final, and it isn't easy to believe that your future with your loved one is gone forever.

## Who am I?

You start to wonder what kind of person you will become.

Maybe be more generous because that was how my daughter lived her life. Of course, it's important to live your life being kind and helpful, but there is always room to do more.

You start wondering, "Who am I?" A grieving person feels very different. You try every day to feel normal, but there is no more normal.

Your world is different. My wife and other children would see the sadness. It becomes a challenge to believe you will be happy again. Of course, you want to return to being that person, but being joyful during this time was hard to envision. So you try to be joyful one moment at a time and appreciate the good things in life.

It was necessary to believe these helpless feelings would im-prove over time. So I turned my destiny over to God and began reading the Bible and more books on Grief to get through this journey. My belief in the afterlife strengthened, especially after reading books on Near Death Experiences from people who have flat-lined and come back to life.

Of course, one hopes to see their loved one again, and it's the one thing to believe in to get well and manage your Grief.

## GRIEVING AND MOURNING

As I read more about Grief, mourning, and specifically depres-sion, I discovered the acute distress lessens over time because the intense chest pressure, dizziness, headaches, and extreme fatigue are less frequent. It was almost four months, and I began to realize and accept this would be a long-term road to recovery. I understood the solid, unavoidable emotions of Grief. Reading the sad and heartbreaking stories of parents losing their child, in a way, helped me accept that these emotions were normal. Although I was still in an acute grieving stage, the emotional outbursts were not as long or debilitating as they once were. I began to understand the differences between mourning com-pared to grieving.

**A definition of mourning:**
*Mourning is a feeling of sadness after a loss. You spend time crying and feeling depressed over the loss. Grieving is more in-ternal and, as mentioned before, has no time limit. Complicated grieving could result in long-term depression. Mourning is more external and involves sharing and outwardly expressing your Grief, maybe by wearing black or opening up to special friends.*

*Reflection:*

My regret over the past year was not pursuing professional counseling, especially counseling for mental trauma. The severe trauma caused shaking nightly for several months. I wish that I had
sought professional help. The intense shaking resulted in dangerously high blood pressure. Looking back, I didn't care about
my health. It was a time when common-sense decisions were
not in my thoughts. A well-known counseling or grieving group
called "Compassionate Friends" would have been an excellent
place to start meeting parents with this same significant loss.
After a year had passed, I was finally ready to connect with this
group. You realize the need to meet and befriend people who
have gone through the same type of loss.

# CHAPTER 22

# APPROACHING FOUR MONTHS

AS I APPROACHED four months since my child died, I started to believe and feel like surrendering to the weight of Grief. You now know to breathe deeply and exhale to calm down. Then as you get up in the morning, you may shed tears and feel better.

You realize the need to regain strength from the lost energy and constant fatigue. So the days improve as you take small steps to recover from the anguish.

You start understanding how physical and mental struggles can overtake and consume the body and mind. My son was doing very well these days and handled adversity much better than me. He understood Grief and saw firsthand what a father goes through when losing a child. He would think about his children and try to envision the pain. He received extensive Grief counseling and kept busy working at his job, doing projects around the house, and raising his family.

My son understood my despair and how losing a child can cause a parent's emotions to become uncontrollable. He felt lost and out of control when Amanda died. There was some guilt, as we all experience when we think back on what could have been done or said to help prevent this tragedy. He felt helpless. I saw his broken heart and the pain in his eyes. My son and I have a lot in common. We know tremendous pain and how it can become a part of our life.

## MAKING SOME PROGRESS

As each day goes by, there is a determination to get well. You take your fight against sadness one day at a time. You have to make that decision, or you will get stuck in Grief, and I understand that getting stuck in Grief leads to long-term depression. Seeing that I was progressing and getting through the acute stages of Grief was vital. After 100-plus days, I still shed tears each day, but I also began to have extended periods of emotional relief. You still feel empty and lonely, but it doesn't consume you as much every minute of the day. So I believed this was my progress through the unwelcome stage of debilitating Grief. There is extreme mental and physical pain and hopelessness that you may experience with extended or complicated Grief. These are complex stages that one should work hard to avoid.

## MY FIRST GRIEVING COUNSELING SESSION DID NOT GO WELL

After all the progress I believed I was making, I decided to attend a grief group through a local church. Finally, I felt ready to listen and speak about my daughter. It was a Zoom call with about 30 people attending. I was in Maryland and most attendees lived in South Carolina, but several people were dialing in from other states. I felt calm, and I listened. I saw Amanda's mom, my former wife, online, and she gave me a wave. At the time, I believed this would be good for me. In earlier weeks, my emotions were out of control. I remembered that emotional breakdown in the hotel lobby in front of 100 people. I would tear up in the car almost every day, wake up every morning in tears, and drop tears most nights before sleep. I didn't care at the time. The pain was so intense that I didn't care what people thought if they saw me in despair.

This time was different. I felt better and was ready to talk about my daughter. So as everybody online took their turn to introduce themselves and mention their loss, I waited my turn. Most people online had lost their spouse, parent, brother, or sister. I didn't hear anyone speak who lost a child. It was emotional for some of the people who discussed their loss. Others spoke easily and unemotionally. I noticed these people online lost their loved ones some years ago. They communicated clearly and frankly. Others whose loss was more recent were a bit more emotional.

Then my turn came up to speak. I said my name and where I lived and had to mention my loss. At that moment, I tried to say, "I lost my daughter four months ago," but the words would not come out. I teared up and couldn't control myself. I couldn't breathe, and my anxiety spiked. It was only four months, and I still experienced lapses in emotions that I could not control. It was embarrassing to me. I felt so weak and disappointed in myself that I could not say, "My daughter died four months ago." The words would not come out! So there I was, broken again in front of people I did not know.

It made me angry inside that this Grief was so intense that it quickly took over my body and mind. It was so frustrating and disappointing that I decided to leave the meeting and turn off the computer.

I thought I knew enough about Grief's strength through reading many books, so the disappointment remained. I needed to reassess myself and think through what else was required to become semi-normal again. You come to realize that you need more time.

Being emotional at a group counseling session was a setback for me, but the realization is that Grief will come at the most unexpected moments, even when you feel you have turned the corner. From my perspective, you have to expect that this may happen to you. The uncontrolled emotions hit you when you least expect them. It is not as acute after time has passed, but it is still there to remind you that you still have to live without your child.

## WHAT THE DAY REALLY FEELS LIKE
## MASKING

After four months, you know that you have to move forward. My family members provided encouragement and became very helpful, and I learned to appreciate the love and the care that embraced me and felt blessed to have that support. I am retired and have time on my hands. Time to think and grieve daily can be a detriment and leaves you with the feeling that time has stopped. Quite honestly, you go through the day feeling like you are carrying that heavy weight on your back and wearing a mask to hide the sorrow on your face. You think you have to fake it and be strong, be happy and appear to be doing fine. The truth is, it's too early to feel okay. Four months into the Grief of losing your child is still the most challenging road to travel.

You love your family and your child, and when you are a man, our culture sees you as weak when you get emotional. Men must keep it together, weather the storm, and leave it behind. Mothers express their emotions more than fathers.

Nevertheless, you know your memories of your loved one will never fade. I spent many months "masking" or suppressing my emotions to give friends and family around me a break from my sadness.

*A quick story to tell*

After I dropped my car off at a dealership for an oil change, my wife drove me back to pick up the vehicle. We drove away separately, and I thought my wife was well ahead of me. When we arrived at our home, she said she pulled up beside me two times without me noticing her. I asked her how I looked. She said that I looked despondent, sad, and gloomy. Looking lost is what it is like when you mask your feelings. I let the mask down when I thought I was alone, and the sadness showed.

I was still in a fog from Grief, which was why I didn't see her pull up beside me at two red traffic lights. Masking is part of Grief.

## Reflection:

Reflecting a year later, you will have many thoughts about moving forward. You will experience all the feelings and emotions during this challenging journey. Your mind becomes your salvation. You think about so many things that have affected your life. You want to get well. You think about medication and your faith, and you may start reading more to understand everything you have experienced. You think about your family, what they have gone through, and how they supported or did not support you. You will mask your emotions. You will wonder how long it will last and fear another tragedy. There will be setbacks; how could there not be disappointments? This is a life journey. Believe me when I say this: It will get better. You will survive, and these negative thoughts and fears will fade.

# CHAPTER 23

# MY DAUGHTER'S HEADSTONE

## MAKING A SELECTION

I visited a local business selling headstones shortly after Amanda died. I walked out of the facility on that first visit because selecting a headstone for Amanda's grave was too difficult at that time. But now, after 4 ½ months, my former wife and I scheduled an appointment to go in and select something for Amanda. I spent several days with high anxiety anticipating this day. Finally, however, we went in and calmly selected a headstone and picked out the size and design. They did not have our first choice, a heart headstone, but it was time to purchase. We selected one with a cross and flowers and birds etched on it. Amanda loved birds; her faith was strong, and she had a heart of gold, so we picked the stone with these items. We also added a wonderful saying to be etched on the back of the stone. Picking out a gravestone is difficult for a bereaved parent. Organizing the details and making a purchase like this becomes an emotional challenge. Although a bereaved parent may become numb to this process, it was essential to stay strong this time. The exhaustion and anticipation of purchasing a gravestone depleted my energy, and no tears were left. The back of the headstone reflects how we all feel.

Missing You Always

You never said I'm leaving
You never said Goodbye.
You were gone before we knew it
And only God knows why.

In life I loved you dearly
In death I love you still,
In my heart I hold a place
That only you can fill.

It broke my heart to lose you
But you didn't go alone.
A part of me went with you
The day God took you home.

## FIRST DOCTOR'S APPOINTMENT AFTER AMANDA'S DEATH

I scheduled my first doctor's appointment as a new patient. Maybe it wasn't a great idea to see a doctor while grieving, but I kept it. My blood pressure and heart rate were always low. I stayed in shape through tennis and exercising daily. However, I hadn't done much of anything since Amanda's death. The doctor was very nice. I filled out all my medical issues and emotional state of mind questions on the form before the appointment, so she knew that I was grieving my daughter's death. Then the doctor took my blood pressure. She seemed puzzled at the first reading. Then she took my blood pressure three more times. It was very high—way too high for it to remain at the levels she was reading. High blood pressure was a first for me, but it didn't surprise me.

The anxiety for over four months and Amanda's death caused physical issues. So now I monitored the levels daily and hoped the numbers would decrease over time.

After speaking with me, the doctor recommended an anti-depressant and additional medicine to calm me down at night. Last, she suggested that a psychiatrist assist me through my Grief and help me manage the medication over time. I noticed that the anti-depressant medicine prescribed included enough refills to last a year. I guess I didn't suppress my Grief well when discussing my daughter. The pain was evident, and the struggle was apparent. Grief is painful. The sadness, anxiety, and need for medicine are all familiar; it is a journey no one would ever want to endure. Later in this book, I will discuss thoughts about medicine and counseling.

## ANXIETY ON VALENTINE'S DAY

Leading up to Valentine's Day, I experienced extreme anxiety for several days. The daily readings from my home blood pressure machine continued to be higher than they should have been. Amanda always remembered me on Valentine's Day. The day usually ended with a nice, friendly call telling me how deep her love was for the whole family.

Amanda would call to share her affectionate feelings. She was always so thoughtful. I would receive cards in the mail once in a while that expressed her appreciation for my support, no matter the circumstances. She always felt thankful that I was there for her. Amanda expressed her love for me, my wife, her mother, and her stepdad in many ways.

# VALENTINE'S DAY – SOCIAL MEDIA POST

Of course, Valentine's Day was special. But this day was also a most challenging time thinking about the past. My wife and I went to dinner at a local restaurant. We noticed a father and his daughter having dinner at a table across from us. It was a precious thing to see. The daughter, about six years old, was wearing a pretty red dress and carried a vase of flowers her dad had given her. It was a beautiful sight to behold. My thoughts turned to what I would have given to spend just one day or even one more hour with my daughter. My wife saw the pain in my eyes as I tried to enjoy this evening. But the Grief within you does not have a schedule when it rears its head. God bless my Amanda on Valentine's Day. I posted this message on social media on Valentine's Day.

Happy Valentine's Day to my dear precious daughter. You are in our hearts forever. We all miss you every day. Remember our special moments on this special day. Love dad

## First-time Dinner with New Friends

We were invited to dinner with some new friends the day after Valentine's Day. My wife did not know the other two couples but had known my one friend for many years. My new friend and his wife were very generous to us by donating to Ellie's "Go Fund Me" account.

They were hosting this wonderful dinner. I was nervous and worried about controlling my emotions, especially in front of these new friends. Drinking a small glass of wine calmed me down. The evening went by, and everyone talked about their families and children. They did not ask me about my family, siblings, or children. Avoiding discussing my children may have been intentional. They realized that it could be emotional for me to discuss Amanda. I was relieved they avoided this conversation because I was not ready to talk about my children at a dinner party that could have turned sad. It was a refreshing evening, but as a bereaved parent, you realize how fragile you are. Grief rears its head in many ways and does get exhausting. The simplest things become a challenge to your mental state. But to me, this was progress. At least I attended the dinner party instead of turning down the invitation. We made new friends, which made my wife happy and gave me a warm feeling that these friends were so kind and generous.

# CHAPTER 24

# TRYING TO STAY BALANCED

## FINDING MIDDLE GROUND

As mentioned earlier, I allowed myself to grieve intensely and felt it was my way of showing love for my daughter. Looking back on my earlier days of Grief, you realize you have no choice and can't control those intense emotions.

It overtakes you in every way you can imagine. No one can help you early on. Nothing will seem to matter. You can't fix this, and no one can help you. Your Grief is intense, and that is what love is. You reach the most profound feelings because your love is so deep. In my fifth month, the intense Grief subsided for me. It didn't end, but you must give your emotions a break.

After a time, you finally get the strength to control your grieving. I was able to choose when to grieve. So it was therapeutic for me to play that song or look at those videos or pictures that would make me emotional. You believe your loved one is watching you. However, the intense grieving subsides over time. You are healing, even if you don't realize it at the time.

What is the middle ground?

Yes, your journey is to get through Grief, not over it, but there is still pain. It may not consume you, but it will always be there. I believe that this is how it should be. You may take a long time to accept the loss of your child in your heart, but you realize that acceptance will not take away the pain. It is now a part of you. It's your restructured life. Once you realize this, life becomes a little easier, knowing that it's a burden you carry for your child's love.

Accepting your child's death is the pain, and this is your middle ground.

## THE ACTUAL DEPTH OF LOVE

The reality is that we will all love and lose several times during our lifetimes. So you think back and try to remember the level of grieving during past difficult times. You remember it was heartfelt and emotional, and maybe you remember being on the verge of an emotional breakdown. I probably experienced some of those.

Past tragedies are a blur. Time doesn't stop. There will always be birthdays and holidays, especially Thanksgiving, when you gather for big family dinners. But when there is a reversal in the order of death, it hits you more profoundly than anyone can imagine.

When you lose a child, the depth of your love reaches intense levels. It is something you have never experienced. Of course, you always loved your child and your children, that is a fact, but there is something about the death of your child that brings out a depth of emotion that is difficult to explain. It is a love that only parents who suffer such a significant loss can experience. So you move forward with a newfound passion for loving harder and more often than ever.

## ELLIE RETURNS FOR A VISIT

We were fortunate to see Ellie about a week for every two months that passed. My former wife had temporary guardianship of Ellie. Early on, Ellie would be my salvation. She was everything I needed to hold on to remember my daughter.

Ellie looked so much like Amanda when she was her age. I enjoyed Ellie this visit; she was even more loving than on the prior visit. Growing up before my eyes, she was a joy.

However, there were sad thoughts of Amanda missing out on Ellie growing up. Amanda would miss raising Ellie and watching her experience all of life's events.

Grief sometimes turns you sideways, so it surprised me to feel the sadness again. But love for Ellie helped tremendously. My thoughts became more positive as time passed. For example, here she is assisting me in watering the garden.

## Ellie missing her mommy

Here is one example of the heartbreak that comes in an instant at times you least expect it. We took Ellie to the park to ride the swings and have fun on the children's slides. There were three other little girls there with their moms. Ellie ran toward them, so excited, and wanted to play. It was all fun to watch. The other girls played with Ellie, laughing, climbing, and swinging. As time passed, the little girls started asking their mommies for various things. Of course, the mothers went over to their children to comfort them and were happy and affectionate with their moms. Ellie just watched the little girls as they went over to their moms.

Ellie glanced at me and gave me a long, sad look as she started to tear up. I felt Ellie's pain as she probably remembered her mom, who wasn't there.

Amanda used to take Ellie to the playground all the time. It was heartbreaking for me to see Ellie missing her mom. I could see it in the expressions on her face. My wife and I quickly attend-ed to Ellie and focused on helping her have more fun at the playground. Seeing a child looking lonely was an instant of sadness and loneliness we experienced five months after losing my daughter.

We have to trust in God to give us all the strength to move through our Grief; even Ellie, at three years old, grieves at times.

### Reflection:

A year later, about thirteen months after her mom's death, Ellie went trick-or-treating Halloween night with Amanda's mother in South Carolina. She enjoyed her time visiting all the homes and gathering treats. But as the night ended and they got in the car, Ellie had a complete meltdown. Her uncontrollable tears overwhelmed her; she was missing her mom. Ellie asked, "Why did other children have their mommy on Halloween when my mommy was not here? I want my mommy back," she cried. "Why can't my mommy come back? Why did her heart break?" These are moments when you realize that children, even at the youngest age, grieve and will experience more sadness as time passes when they remember more about what happened. It is heartbreaking to see a child suffer during these difficult times.

# CHAPTER 25

# THAT PARTICULAR DATE – UNEXPECTED EMOTIONS

## FIVE-MONTH ANNIVERSARY

We believe Amanda died on September 26th. Her stepdad found her lifeless on the floor of her apartment on the 27th. He drove to the apartment because she was not answering her phone the night of the 26th or the following day. These dates are etched permanently in my mind.

After five months, it all remained a blur. The days go from moving slowly to flying by at times. But life continues, and people move forward with their daily routines. My other daughter continued to be emotional most days, and I tried to comfort her, but sometimes you must let the grieving flow. All I could do was tell her it would take time. I thought, *Why should I try to stop my other daughter from crying when it is difficult for me to do the same?* It was important to stay resilient in front of my other children because it was a family crisis.

## UNEXPECTED MELTDOWNS

As the weeks passed, I rarely remembered the days, and the nights seemed to pass without knowing what I did that day. Still feeling better but somewhat numb and alone, I thought I was on a good path. My emotions receded and became more controllable.

A story to tell: It was tax season. On this day, I drove to my accountant's office to deliver my tax forms for the year. I had mentioned Amanda's death to my accountant a few months earlier. When I returned the papers to the receptionist, my accountant came out of the office to greet me. The receptionist proceeded to the back room to give us some privacy.

My accountant was compassionate, and she asked what had happened. It had been a while since someone asked me that question. I did not know her well since I had just moved from South Carolina to Maryland. As I discussed Amanda and how she died, I welled up in tears. I talked about my struggles and my family. She was very consoling and understood my despair. I thanked her and appreciated her compassion and advice. My main point here is to let you know that Grief has a life of its own, and you realize you have a long way to go on your Grief journey.

You realize that you will go in and out of acute Grief the first year of your loss and maybe into the second or third year. Being a bereaved parent is the cross you bear, and you will have to carry this for the rest of your life.

## UNEXPECTED REFLECTION – AMANDA'S SCENT

The mind works in mysterious ways when you are grieving. You come across things, events, and places that remind you of your lost child. For example, Amanda's car was brought up from South Carolina to Maryland and given to Ellie's father. It sat idle over the winter, and I helped him get a new battery and start the car.

As I sat in Amanda's car, I smelled her scent. Inhaling Amanda's scent created a rush of memories and a rush of sadness. It reminded me how many things you remember about your child, even their scent. Of course, you never think of these things when your child is alive, but you pray every day that there will always be something to remind you of your child. It sounds a bit crazy, but you are not crazy.

You have enhanced senses when you grieve, and everything magnifies. Your awareness becomes acute, and you search for anything to relieve your broken heart. As I looked inside Amanda's car, I saw some remaining items. My child would be gone forever, but the memories would never fade. When I returned home, I kept some of Amanda's clothes, including her favorite blue jumper outfit. The aroma in the car and on her clothes remained the same. I knew that she was always with me. Enhanced senses and reminders are a daily occurrence; this is how bereaved parents live after losing their precious child.

## THE SONG OF ALL SONGS: "WHAT CHILD IS THIS?"

In my fifth month, I was progressing well toward normalcy. However, all days are different. We received a nice gift for Christmas from my stepdaughter and her husband. They gave us a beautiful clock that chimed instrumental Christmas tunes at the top of each hour. I didn't know why, but this song resonated with me. The song was "What child is this."

It was a way for me to remember and acknowledge that my child was in the arms of Jesus.

Any parent who has lost a child may feel a connection to their loved one by listening to this song. This song should be for all the sons and daughters who have lost their lives. This links to the original version of "What Child is this."

Reference https://www.youtube.com/watch?v=kQWKjTvPgiM

# CHAPTER 26

# HOPING FOR REMISSION FROM GRIEF

IT WAS SIX months to the day that my daughter died. There had been silent days and times when I felt normalcy was around the corner. I haven't written much about how my wife handled this tragedy. My wife, Amanda's stepmom, loved Amanda like she was her child. Then, one night, my wife fell out of bed in the middle of the night. She internalized her Grief, became anxious, and kept almost everything inside. My wife cried many times over the first six months. Over all this time, she experienced sleepless nights and constant nightmares. It was the stress from my Grief, the tension in the family dealing with all our Grief, and she showed a sadness that she could not hide. So I asked myself, was she doing well?

A couple of days later, my wife fell out of bed again, resulting in significant bruises and welts on her back, ribs, and leg. Her stress was still evident six months after my daughter died. I mention this because anxiety and sleepless nights may continue, even when things seem to be getting better. I would fall asleep rocking side to side until I could no longer remember moving. It became a crutch for me to calm my internal anxiety. Unfortunately, the restlessness disrupted my wife's sleep, as she rarely could sleep beyond two hours throughout the night.

So it was time for me to stay calm and suppress the thoughts. Unfortunately, Grief has a mind of its own. It controls you, and you have to pray it will end someday.

## MAJOR SETBACKS DO OCCUR

As I have mentioned, you may have significant setbacks in your recovery from losing your child, and difficulties in your marriage or other relationships. At times during extended Grief, you feel helpless and out of control. You feel weakness in dealing with the unrelenting feelings of sadness and hopelessness.

Reading and writing help, but in the end, there will be difficulty in accepting the death of your child. So you reassess yourself and figure out the steps you must take to get well. At times, you will feel like you are starting over. It becomes frustrating and upsetting, in ways no one could imagine. Finally, I asked myself, "Who am I?" My wife asked me, "Who are you? I don't recognize who you are."

You feel like a stranger within, changed forever. At this time in my journey, I changed for the worse, at least temporarily. So you start over, make amends, and try to regain the energy lost during conflict and difficult days. Just be aware that you may not be the person you want to be, but you have to pray for the strength to become that better person you used to be.

## LOOKING FOR SOLITUDE AND SERENITY

After a setback in my recovery, I turned to my shaken faith for more strength. I started to drive around aimlessly with empty thoughts. Finally, I went to a place called Cunningham Falls.

*Reference https://travel.sygic.com/en/poi/cunningham-falls-state-park-poi:2456600*

*Cunningham Falls State Park is a public recreation area located west of Thurmont, Maryland, in the United States. The state park is the home of Cunningham Falls, the largest cascading waterfall in Maryland, and a 43-acre man-made lake. The park is one of several protected areas occupying the 50-mile-long Catoctin Mountain; it is bordered on its north by Catoctin Mountain Park and on its south by Frederick Municipal Forest.*

This historic man-made lake provided enjoyable activities for families and solitude for those seeking peace.

It was a cloudy day in early April. I drove to the park and found myself alone in the large parking lot; nobody was there. As I was resting in my car, clouds started moving in, and it began to rain. Surprisingly, it started to sleet, and then, to my amazement, it began to hail.

There was an immediate change in the weather. I enjoyed seeing my car covered with little white balls of hail while looking out at the lake. Appreciating nature was a moment that brought me peace, alone in an empty park.

Then in an instant, the clouds separated, and the sun began to shine. It was April, not December, but I will never forget this moment. It brought the calmness of solitude and the peacefulness of serenity.

In my fragile state of mind, seeing the sun and new warmth brought thoughts of hope and joy for my future. Those who have felt the deep trauma of loss can understand how Grief can lead to an appreciation of nature.

## Going fishing with my son and grandchildren

My son invited me to go fishing with three of his children. Initially, I felt a solid resistance to accepting. However, it would be good for me to create memories with my son and grandchildren and stop turning down compassionate invites from family and friends. It was time to continue to move forward. It may seem weak and silly to read this. But why would it be so hard to go fishing and be with family?

It is about getting past exhaustion, mental strain, and finality. Therefore, it was essential to carry on and find joy while carrying sadness. A bereaved parent realizes this is their life and the life of anyone who lost a child.

The day ended in joy. It was a happy, memorable time fishing with family, and it may have been the beginning of getting past the acute Grief, relieving some of the sadness, and enjoying some precious moments in life.

## Soon after Easter Sunday: A
### golden finch appears

Almost seven months since Amanda's passing, I decided to sit and have lunch by her gravesite. Sitting there near her was challenging, yet without her; it was a lonely moment. Sipping on coffee and having a sandwich reminded me of my visits to her apartment, enjoying coffee and breakfast together. I remember bursting with pride watching her nurturing and loving little Ellie; she was so happy being her mom. These are the memories I will miss, forever.

The following day, my wife and I sat on our front porch, thinking of the finality of it all. I wished for relief from the anxiety of wondering if my daughter was safe and happy. At that moment, we saw a goldfinch that landed on the tree in front of us. The bird was spectacular! It turned and looked at us for a few moments, then flew away. My wife wondered what it meant to see a goldfinch. It is not common to see a yellow finch in Maryland. Nevertheless, there is a spiritual meaning to seeing this beautiful bird.

What does it mean to see a goldfinch?

*Reference https://www.sonomabirding.com/goldfinch-symbolism/*

*The goldfinches are symbolic of joy, enthusiasm, positivity, and persistence. In Christianity, these birds have a strong symbolism and are considered sacred. In ancient Egyptian culture, goldfinches personify the souls of dead human beings.*

*But that's not all these birds represent. They also symbolize enthusiasm and liveliness. These birds are always bursting with energy as long as they live.*

*The spirit of the goldfinches also symbolizes optimism. These birds believe in always looking at the bright side of things.*

# PART 2

## REFLECTIONS

# CHAPTER 27

# THOUGHTS OVER THE FOLLOWING MONTHS

AFTER EXPERIENCING ACUTE Grief, your mind turns toward many thoughts about every conceivable subject you have not experienced before. Part 2 of this book captures these thoughts and reflections about the emotions of Grief following my child's death. You see a change in family and friends and embrace how they have supported you. I started seeing a difference in my children, primarily good changes.

You think about turning toward the future because you want to heal. However, if you are married or have a significant other, you realize your relationship loses energy during these challenging times.

If you are single, you know that it becomes a lonelier road to bear. You debate attending counseling and whether it will be beneficial for you. You will experience and fully understand unpleasant grieving emotions, such as sadness, distress, suffering, misery, and agony.

These emotions turn into better days and positive feelings about your life, and you will move forward with conviction. You may not think this is true in the early days of Grief, but strength comes when you do the right things and make the best decisions for yourself.

I will share other thoughts in the following chapters. You will con-tinue to reflect on many things. You imagine all the "what-if" scenarios that flood your mind because you may have regrets or guilt. The peak of sadness comes when you realize you must say goodbye. You will continue searching for facts and wonder what your purpose is on this earth. You question everything because you are in a world of confusion. Getting through the first year takes more courage than you could ever imagine. You may have to explain and help people understand how you feel. With time you realize that you have to start taking care of yourself.

These chapters explain what I experienced. These are challeng-ing times. As you progress, drained and exhausted, you will have pain and ailments you never experienced before.

As time passes, you'll see that things do get better. You realize that Grief is all-encompassing, and you start to notice a change in people's demeanor. Once you understand this painful journey, you will rise with more strength than you ever imagined. You will survive to live your life again with your child on your shoulders.

When your child is born, you become a parent. When your child dies, you become a bereaved parent. Your child was a part of you when you became a parent, and now he or she is a part of you as a bereaved parent. It is a cross to bear; you will carry your loss with a newfound strength.

You may assess your physical, mental, and emotional wellness toward the end of the first year. You may emerge from initial suicidal thoughts to wanting to live. You start thinking about your mortality. If you are a Christian, you revisit whether you have been faithful to God in the past or never devoted. You may start believing in heaven, believing in God, because you will do anything to see this special place to see your child again. You have a broken heart and begin to understand what this tragedy has done to damage it.

There is a difference in how you feel when you lose other family members and then lose your child. The pain of losing a child is beyond one's comprehension.

You may have feelings of resentment toward things that you never expected. I discuss this in the following chapters. Your days feel like you are wearing a mask and pretending to be well. Group therapy or professional counseling is a personal decision, and I share my views. Finding someone or a group who has lost a child may be your best alternative. It is one avenue that is worth a try. As time passes, you may fear another tragedy or losing another child. It happens, and the fear is real. You feel that you can't handle one more tragedy.

Your time is priceless.

You set aside time for reflections and memories and become a person in more profound thought. Make time to be completely quiet every day, if only for 20 minutes. It is healthy to engage in daily routines and activities. Your emotions are on high alert, and this becomes part of you. Then there is the dilemma of a father's Grief. Culture looks upon our Grief differently than that of women. Everybody is different, and we are all grievers, whether a mother or a father. It's called shadow Grief, and it is a term that is used in many books to describe our Grief.

But there is light and sunrise in the mornings ahead. So you start to learn about gratitude and appreciation for small things.

Your health becomes more critical, and you start caring about your appearance. You don't care what you look like for the first six months because Grief drains you emotionally and physically. I share my thoughts on searching for faith and searching for that solitude that is hard to find. There will always be emotional moments, and that is the truth. No one can make us feel better, but we must do everything we can to cherish and live a life with joy and fond memories.

# CHAPTER 28

# ASSESSING MY STATE OF MIND AFTER SEVEN MONTHS

SEVERAL ACTIVITIES HELPED me avoid long-term depression. All the reading, writing, and sports activities helped sideline my emotions temporarily, but at the end of the day, you still realize that your child is not with you anymore. You try to keep busy working on projects, doing chores, and initially joining a group counseling session or two. But at the end of each day, your world feels lonely and helpless.

So you admit that your life will have to continue without your child, which is difficult for any bereaved parent to accept. Every morning you wake up with a touch of happiness, but that quickly turns to sadness when you realize this was more than a nightmare.

The energy loss and the thought of living in a different world can be overwhelming. There were periods during the first seven months when I believed better days were ahead. You trust you are doing all the right things in managing your Grief. But even when you think you are doing all the right things, the Grief still consumes you; you just learn to handle the sorrow.

There is one thing that helps you heal. There is nothing more powerful than love for your child. Love is everything. Love was my way out of this Grief, and that love was the energy source needed to start enjoying life without my daughter.

Seven months was not enough time to get through my Grief. There was not much anyone could do or say to make me feel better. It takes time to heal your heart.

Be prepared for the long journey. Several books on Grief indicated that it might take bereaved parents 2-5 years to feel emotionally balanced. Unfortunately, it may take that long, even when you think you are doing everything right.

Physically, in early Grief, you may feel dizzy on many occasions and become unbalanced. Sometimes I would lose my balance, bump into walls, drop things constantly and not even remember what I had done that day. The physical and mental toll Grief takes on you can be demoralizing. Be patient with yourself; your physical health improves with time.

## WHAT IS NEEDED TO GET BEYOND THE ACUTE GRIEF?

So how did I get beyond the acute Grief? The truth is, I wasn't out of this critical phase in my seventh month. You prepare to ride the wave of Grief and trust God to heal in good time. I was submissive to the strength of Grief. It is not something that you can fight through, avoid or ignore. Once you accept that this is your new journey, then it becomes just a little bit easier to bear. Once you accept it, there are no surprises. You will be sabotaged by Grief at unexpected moments. You will become emotional when you least expect it.

So I moved forward, willing to shed tears and be prepared for the unexpected. I was at peace knowing that carrying sorrow was normal for a bereaved parent. Only a bereaved mother or father could genuinely understand the emotions one goes through.

Finding solitude and meeting someone who could share and understand the intense pain was essential. I engaged in privacy and being alone. When the pain becomes too much to bear, you may continue to search for someone else who lost a child or loved one.

## TAKING THAT VACATION IS NOT THE BEST CHOICE

Wishing the pain to end, I considered taking a long vacation to clear my mind and 'get away from it all'. Maybe a long trip somewhere in the United States.

Then I read a story about a mother who decided to tour Europe for a few weeks with her husband after their child died. The results weren't favorable. She saw all the fantastic sights one would see on such a vacation. It was excruciatingly painful for her. It exacerbated their pain and their loneliness, as they missed their child. They were in a fog. They spent a great deal of money on an empty vacation and did not remember much of anything. I surmised that perhaps engaging in many activities and keeping manically busy to try to 'forget,' does not work. It just delays your reality and perhaps becomes a journey that takes you down a longer, more difficult path.

You may feel, as I did, that you are not getting better even though your child has been gone for many months. You can get involved in dozens of activities if you think being more active would help you heal. However, when you try to avoid Grief, it delays your pain. You accept that this will be a difficult journey.

During the first year, you learn that the choices you make during Grief, choices about time, commitments, activities, and behavior, must be faced and then journeyed through. Avoiding Grief during the first year delays your pain; accept that this will be a difficult journey. For those with Faith in God, prayers for wisdom and strength to persevere, offer solace. Others, may find comfort in finding a listening ear to discuss the need for willpower to get through this most difficult time.

## FIVE DAYS AWAY FROM HOME

In May, eight months after Amanda's passing, my wife and I decided to take a short trip. My stepson, from LA, was on assignment, filming a documentary in Florida. After a few days there, I began feeling lost, far from 'home'; far from Amanda's gravesite.

As weak and absurd as it sounds, being 'far from Amanda' consumed my thoughts and set me back somewhat in my grieving progress. I was glad to spend time with my stepson, whom I hold great admiration for, watching him steadfastly follow his dreams, despite all obstacles. I have gained strength in observing his proven resilience over the years. But, at the same time, it was the first time spending a great distance from my daughter's grave, and I realized that Grief does not end with distance.

You realize and start to believe that time is on your side and that you must face the pain to relieve the pain. You look around and see other people's resilience, like my stepson, and it strengthens you. You may not believe the pain lessens over time, but it does if you stay firm in your belief that your child is safe and out of any pain they may have experienced in their last days.

## LONELINESS

Returning from my short trip, I immediately visited the cemetery to see my child. It was a relief to be close to her even though she was gone. The tears flowed again, but I felt better sitting there reflecting on more positive thoughts. However, loneliness filled my mind. A bereaved parent will reflect on how their family has changed. You reflect on some of the positive changes to heal your heart.

There comes a time when you must stop thinking about what you have lost and start thinking about the needs of the people around you.

One of the most effective ways to escape loneliness is to reach out to others who have also lost a child or are just hurting or in need. You reach out even if you don't feel like reaching out. It takes strength and discipline to do it anyway.

It takes work. You cannot do it overnight. For some people, reaching out may take months.

In my eighth month after Amanda died, I wanted to move forward and reach out to anyone who had lost a child.

It was time to begin thinking about other people's needs. People want to see you happy. They do not want to see you sad. They want to feel comfortable with you. Yet there is an uneasiness about it all.

You know you are unhappy inside; you know you are lonely. You have to move forward and live a semi-normal life again. It becomes so unhealthy to wallow in self-pity. It will bring you to the brink of long-term depression that may never end. So now you

rely on family and friends to support you. You become determined to keep trying to do the right things for yourself.

The need to accept your most traumatic fear finally sets in.

You are a different person inside.

Others may see you as recovered as you force yourself to mask
the pain that will always be in your broken heart.

But someday, you will find the pain easing. At least you will pray
for that day. Then you will continue to carry your child's shadow
everywhere you go to feel your child's strength. It will help you
move forward with joy and happiness in your child's memory.

## WHERE ARE YOU, MY CHILD?

During the second half of the first year, my thoughts turned toward wondering, *Where is my child?* These are very intense moments for a bereaved parent. Whether you are a Christian or an
atheist, the deepest thoughts of a parent who has lost a child are
where their child is. You think about this intensely many times
over the first year. Where is my child? Most parents believe their
child is in Heaven, safe and out of pain, especially if they believe
in Heaven.

But I would ask myself, *Where is she? Can my child hear me
when I speak? Can she see me when I look up at the sky? Can
she see my anguish, and can she see my pain?*

*How does she look? Does she look like I last saw her? Is she a
spirit? What is her human form, if any form? Is she in darkness,*

*in oblivion?* Maybe you wonder if your child is happy or lost in a dark world.

When a person goes under anesthesia, they don't remember a thing when they wake up. Is that how it is? You wonder about these things when you realize your child is gone. In most religions, the belief is that there is a more heartwarming place, and your spirit lives on. But when you are traumatized from your child's death, you fall deep into thought and question where your child may be and wonder if your child is safe. We all want our children to be happy and safe.

If a Christian, a bereaved parent wants to believe their child has entered the gates of Heaven. They are now loving spirits with God in the most incredible place imaginable. That is what we pray. But these moments occur when you look down at your child's grave, only four feet away from you, and one can only think, *Where is my child?*

## Grief slowly builds, then you release

There does come a time when you have to wipe away the tears. At least you wish the tears could stop someday to give you some relief. By the end of the eighth month, I learned to mask daily and became more aware of the people around me. You are finally able to control your emotions and avoid public meltdowns. But it is challenging to hold it all in. You become a shadow, walking around with the hollowness of a ghost. The broken heart does not go away. Sometimes you feel the buildup of sadness and need to be alone.

So I decided to return to a place of solitude, Cunningham Falls. I bought that Coleman stove all campers desire, packed some food and drinks, brought a book to read, and was on my way to the park. It was a short drive from my home. I arrived and set up a chair in front of the water.

There were others present in the picnic areas surrounding me. I sat there, reflecting on how my life and family changed with the death of Amanda.

My eyes welled up for four hours.

I was not crying out of control, but constant tears flowed as I read a book on Grief by the author Gary Roe. I wondered what the other people thought as they looked at a man sitting alone at a lake for hours, barely moving. There was a need to release the Grief that had built up over the past few weeks. It was time for me to be emotional again to show my daughter that I still missed her.

Have you ever had tears flowing for four hours straight? When you think about that, I imagine that not many people have shed tears that long without interruption. Yet, when you lose a child, the tears flow so quickly and easily that you reach an emotional point humans rarely experience.

My main point is this: Sometimes masking and being able to control your emotions is fine. However, it does build up, and the more you suppress it, the longer it takes to get through the Grief. Tears do not dry up when you are sad. You remind yourself that this is a normal human emotion and release those tears in honor of your lost child. Sometimes you need that private moment or that solitude to get through those problematic episodes of despair.

## I WOULD GIVE EVERYTHING I OWN

Sometimes you have to wonder, and you will be surprised when reminders cross your path as you grieve during trying times.

My wife and I decided to visit a 57-acre farm in the foothills of Frederick, Maryland. It was a fabulous nursery filled with thousands of beautiful flowers, plants, and shrubs. On-site, it included several stores with all kinds of knickknacks, pottery, and locally made decorative items. Music was playing throughout the small stores, separated by the different types of items on sale. In addition, there was a band and several food trucks surrounded by many friendly people.

As we shopped and casually looked at all the beautiful items in the store, we saw a tiny angel lying, sound asleep, on a small table near other significant artifacts. We looked at each other and had the same feelings. This angel was an excellent item that would remind us of Amanda. The angel was small enough to fit in the palm of your hand. As I picked it up, thinking of Amanda, a song came on speaker right in front of me.

It was the song by the band Bread *titled*, *"I would give anything I own, just to have you again."*

*I would give anything I own*
*Give up my life, my heart, my home*
*I would give everything I own*
*Just to have you back again*

*Reference https://www.youtube.com/watch?v=2i43aAn2rq8*

These moments bring tears. When you hear a powerful song that resonates with you and reminds you of your love for your child, you know you would give up anything to have your child back; it overwhelms you with tears of love and loneliness. If you are a grieving parent, play this song on YouTube. Not all lyrics apply to your lost child, but that doesn't matter.

The song is actually about the songwriter's father, but the message is the same. If you have ever loved and lost, this video will connect you with your child in the best possible way, and the tears will flow. Remember that tears help you heal. It is another process to help us get through life and Grief. There is no shame in showing tears of love for your child.

You will show how much you miss and love your child as you listen to this song.

## FATHER'S DAY

Family can be a great crutch when those holidays or special days come and go. Father's Day is when Amanda did something special. She always expressed to me that I was the best dad. Most fathers get the pleasure of enjoying their children on Father's Day. I spent a wonderful day with my son, his wife, and my five grandchildren.

The day was enjoyable. The sadness stayed away for the day. However, the memories of Amanda reentered my mind as we drove home from a nice picnic in the park. Of course, it was a difficult day, but I enjoyed my time that day and believed I was turning a corner to feel normal again. At least as normal as a parent can be after losing a child.

I retrieved an e-mail Amanda sent to me years ago. These are the types of memories a bereaved parent embraces and never forgets. These are her words;

*Good morning dad,*

*How are you?*
*I wanted to write you an email.*
*Right now, I'm at Starbucks drinking my favorite chai tea.*
*It has been forever since I've been here. Starbucks was the first thing I cut out of my budget, but I missed it.*
*I couldn't sleep last night and decided to get up at 5 am.*
*Anyways, I want you to know how much I love you.*
*Every time you help me through my rough patches, I never forget who helped me.*
*Your support means so much to me, and I hope you know how great a dad you are.*
*I hope you enjoy your day today and give me a call later if you can, or I'll call you.*
*I love you; I love you; I love you!!!!!!!!*

Two examples of my favorite presents I received from Amanda showed her love, affection, respect, and appreciation of her dad. In addition, she showed love, respect, and gratitude for her whole family. As a bereaved parent, you will cherish all your child's gifts received over the years.

## PHYSICAL AILMENTS OR PAIN CAN IGNITE EMOTIONS

A bereaved parent can feel crazy or out of control and become emotional at unpredictable times. Of course, you expect sadness or tears. Still, when you are mentally drained and have a physical ailment, such as a headache, a stomachache, foot pain, back pain, or anything insignificant, suddenly, those emotions reemerge.

I experienced this many times.

When you are ailing physically, the mental anguish comes back; you reflect on your loss, and it becomes another moment of frustration. It becomes frustrating but also welcomed.

When you have an ailment, as minor as it might be, it stops you and creates a period when you must realize again that your child is gone. It is normal to be this way. At least, you hope that you are not feeling crazy again.

When will it all end? As I have mentioned many times, nobody knows if or when it will ever end. But you have to believe it will get better and less painful, and your resilience strengthens. You recognize signs of progress, remembering that it is a marathon and not a short race to wellness.

# CHAPTER 29

# FAMILY AND FRIEND RELATIONSHIPS

WHEN SADNESS AND joy are intertwined, having the support of family and friends will help you in many ways. I have been fortunate to have a loving family support network. Family support will help you heal and move forward positively in your Grief. Friends and family helped me during emotional times. Knowing they cared and offered support at some of the most appropriate times was heartwarming.

You also will discover that your energy gradually increases, and your mind turns to positive thoughts. If you have other children, reaching out to them and supporting them becomes essential. They need you even if you don't have any strength left. It gave me a sense of comfort and gratitude when other family members called to see how I was doing. You will have periods when you desire to be alone in solitude, but knowing others care helps you realize that many good, loving people surround you. If you do not have family or a few friends, you have your faith. You gain strength through the belief that you will see your child again.

You learn not to judge people for their response or lack of it. People may feel uncomfortable when dealing with a grieving person or couple. Of course, friends and family have good intentions. However, the one thing that made me feel better was receiving heartfelt cards and words of support and acknowledging how difficult this was for our family.

A special card I received contained these words:

> While the rest of the world carries on as though nothing has happened, remember that others know your world will never be the same.

Phone calls were comforting when friends and family said hello and asked if there was anything they could do to help. Most people know what to say and what not to say. Everyone is compassionate. On the other hand, friends and sometimes family members mean well, but the words may be hurtful. Some suggestions I received from friends and family hurt because your senses are magnified when grieving. Your feelings are on high alert, and you may take things the wrong way, but you realize that everyone is just trying to help. Therefore, I was not offended when someone spoke unintentionally insensitive words.

Some friends and family may disappear after an initial support offering. That is okay because people have to move forward in their lives; you can't expect people to continue consoling you for extensive periods. It becomes counterproductive to be reminded of your loss constantly. It is a problematic scenario.

Life is too short to carry resentment. Forgiveness is the only way to move forward and heal from Grief. New friends will emerge, and some family members may provide comfort and support. On the other hand, some longtime friends may disappear, and some longtime friends you haven't seen or heard from in years will become a part of your life. There is always a balance of people, friends, and family that you have to consider. You want to keep and bring new friends into your life who provide energy, not those who exhaust your energy.

Life is precious, and we go through this life one time. Therefore, it is vital to make the necessary changes to keep stress low and positive feelings high. If friends do not contact you in the first year of your Grief, assume they helped provide the space you needed to grieve.

## NOTICING A CHANGE IN PEOPLE'S DEMEANOR

Friends and family sometimes avoided the subject of my child's death. Avoiding the topic is okay because you believe friends and family want you to feel better. Bringing up my child brought sadness in the past. But early on, there is nothing to stop the sadness.

People want you to feel normal and re-emerge as the person you were before. Yet you know in your heart that you are changed forever.

During family visits, relatives wanted to focus on the day's activities, have fun, and enjoy each other's company. Why bring up your child and sadden the day? I understood this completely. Avoidance is normal. Why not try to enjoy a birthday or holiday or just a day's visit? There is a certain uncomfortable feeling in people when talking about death and grave loss. However, you learn to adjust your approach based on the conversation with that person. Inside your heart, you know getting to this place called joy is a struggle, and you try hard to enjoy the moments. For a brief time, there is joy and happiness, and you see that people are living their lives as before. They move on with their everyday lives. Yet you know that your heart is still in pieces, and you cannot fully enjoy the happy events in your life as you did before your child died. You realize that your Grief will take time, and you are only starting to climb that mountain toward normalcy.

My demeanor changed toward being more emotional. A friend of mine traveled to Florida to assist his mother-in-law in caring for her husband because he fell and broke his hip. He shared other serious medical concerns, and my friend was there for a few weeks. When he returned, I asked him how his father-in-law was doing, and he said he had died. I started tearing up immediately, and he quickly changed the subject, probably because we were just about to go onto the tennis court to play some doubles with the guys. You change by feeling more compassion; your emotions are magnified and sometimes not controllable. My heart sank for my friend when he told me about his father-in-law. My feelings were extreme and occasionally unpredictable during this time.

# CHAPTER 30

# EVERYBODY CHANGES IN SOME WAY

MY WHOLE FAMILY changed, including my siblings, son and daughter, stepchildren, and wife. Some changes were good, and some were a bit unexpected. As we all continue to grieve, you realize that everyone grieves differently. You cannot judge how people suffer or react to Grief. Some grieve silently, some outwardly, and some keep busy because it's the only thing they know to move forward and be normal again. The death of a child has heartbreaking consequences for a sister, a brother, an aunt, an uncle, stepchildren, and especially for stepparents and, of course, you as your child's mother or father. There may be reasons for unexpected responses or lack of answers. Everyone has expectations, and sometimes there will be disappointment, but you realize that everyone means well.

## SEEING THE CHANGE IN MY CHILDREN

There were changes in my children and stepchildren that warmed my heart. The death of your child affects all family members. Siblings also grieve with heartbreaking moments and memories. There is guilt and sorrow. They long for forgiveness for anything they did in the past that may have caused sadness to their sister. They pray for forgiveness to feel better and move on with their lives.

## My son

One story to share: My son attended Grief counseling sessions weekly. He has always been a helper, but after his sister's death, he dedicated himself to overcoming difficult times. My son is a senior recruiter for the Intelligence Community, working for a private firm. He is an expert in finding rare talent with rare skills and highly required security clearances. In addition, he is an expert resume writer who has reviewed thousands of resumes over a 14-year career.

He understands the essential hiring methods and how to succeed in an effective interview. So he offered his services to everyone in his group and posted his services to help those in other meetings. The group's main concern was keeping their job or searching for another position. Some lost their jobs due to difficulties dealing with Grief. Some desired a job change or a less stressful work environment. So he offered his services to help them with their resumes and lead them to job openings matching their workforce skills. Coordinating this was time-consuming.

There was compassion in my son to help others. This act of kindness brought tears to my eyes. My son had a full-time job, a family of five children, and many home projects. Yet he compassionately offered his time to help friends from his Grief counseling meetings. His generosity was heartwarming to see as one positive effect of my daughter's death. Why would this bring tears to one's eyes? It's the strength of Grief that makes you more human.

## MY STEPDAUGHTER

My stepdaughter is a loving, caring person who had difficulty accepting Amanda's loss. They enjoyed a unique sibling relationship even though they lived in different states. She felt extreme pain with the loss of her stepsister. She loved Amanda's three-year-old daughter Ellie and showed compassion and generosity. My stepdaughter and her husband gave generous gifts to Ellie during their visits and the holidays. They made a three-hour trip to visit us when we cared for Ellie. I asked myself, *Has my stepdaughter changed?* Only for the better—she has always been emotional and compassionate; the times she had success in her work life, she expressed her love through gifts. She connects in ways that show she understands the despair in our family.

My wife and stepdaughter talk on the phone almost daily, and their close mother-daughter relationship has helped my wife gain more strength to deal with all the emotional days. You will realize that bonding with other family members will help your heart to heal.

## MY DAUGHTER

My younger daughter experienced some unjustified guilt a sister may feel when her sibling dies. She blamed herself for things that didn't make sense. A sibling's guilt feelings are widespread. But over time, she began to realize that nothing she said directly affected the cause of her sister's death.

My daughter watched videos of her sister and read her Bible notes and notebooks. She realized that Amanda had strong faith, and she would sing Christian songs with her. After many weeks and months of crying, my daughter began to find strength and belief that her sister was in heaven and was now in a safe, painless place. Amanda always encouraged her to be strong, have self-respect, and work hard in her job. So she started living in her sister's memory and wanted to move forward as Amanda wanted her to live. As a result, my daughter worked harder at her job, prayed more often, still let her emotions flow, and realized that self-respect for herself and respect for others was Amanda's way of life. She intended to live her life the same way.

## Marriage Impacts – Relationship Impacts

Statistics show that marriage and relationships are at high risk of failure during intense Grief, depending on which studies you read. However, marriages and relationships survive when couples understand Grief. Communication is most important in any relationship but doubly important when tragedy strikes. During the days following the loss of my daughter, my wife wept more than I had ever seen before. After many weeks, we both needed a temporary emotional break due to uncontrolled sadness. I felt the need to be alone to grieve and figure out a way to move forward without leaving destruction all around. We were not in a good place emotionally. Of course not—how could we be? So what can you do to heal and save a marriage or a relationship? I realized changes were needed to show appreciation for everything my wife did behind the daily routines. She kept everything in order around the house, such as doing all the laundry, cooking the meals, taking care of Ellie, being a caring stepmom to my daughter when she was sick, and maintaining our household.

I would spend time alone to grieve without feeling guilty. Unfortunately, this results in the need to take a break from Grief.

Taking a break from grieving will save your heart from breaking beyond repair. So it became essential to stay the course and remain resilient. A tragedy like this, or any tragedy, should not ruin a relationship with your spouse, family, or friends because you realize that you will need people and their compassion moving forward.

# CHAPTER 31

# FINDING SOME HOPE

## FINDING THE PROPER SUPPORT FOR YOU

There is a solid need to deal with all the intense, uncontrollable emotions. There is shock and trauma when you first hear of losing your child. Then you carry the extreme physical and emotional pain for many weeks, months, and maybe years. The sadness and loneliness result when you finally gain the courage to accept your loss. There is anger and questioning God and His purpose, and then you question your purpose.

Accepting the death of a child leads to distress, suffering, misery, and agony when dealing with this enormous, significant loss.

Surprisingly, some people don't get the help they need but somehow survive and continue living their lives in a manageable way. Other people get extensive support through individual or group counseling and find happiness, while others never get through extreme Grief. That is the truth.

For my Grief, I prayed that the pain would finally recede. It would be best if you believed you could do all the right things to survive and be happy again. To this day, I continue to grieve but in a different way. The Grief didn't end with me finishing this book. But I will look back someday, read my book and realize everyone has challenges in life and tragedies to endure.

## COUNSELING THOUGHTS – GOOD OR NOT GOOD

Counseling is a good option most of the time, but it also can go sideways. I did not pursue individual counseling in the first year. However, I intended to keep an open mind if the pain, anxiety, and sadness continued during the second year.

I have friends who did not go to counseling because they did most of the talking and received little feedback that they felt helped them. Many counselors follow the book on grieving and go through the stages and typical timelines. You don't need to be on a timeline.

You quickly learn that grieving has a personal timeline for everyone. Unfortunately, no one can counsel us out of it. You will hear all the things people may have read about grieving your loss, and it can help, but it is essential to find something personal that you can participate in to help you manage your loss.

Experts mention that you should not discount counseling but that it is essential to find the counselor that is right for you. In addition, there must be comfort and a connection with a professional counselor for the sessions to be helpful.

We all migrate toward counseling for many different emotions to help us deal with life in general.

You never expect a child's death, which is debilitating when it occurs. You are unprepared, and the shock and trauma set in.

My goal, even after many months of grieving, was to survive. But you know it will be a challenging and long journey.

Sometimes we may say or do things that result from the stress and anxiety that are unintentional but hurtful.

You hope that the anxiety subsides with the belief that the pain and suffering will someday end. However, there will always be a level of sadness in your heart. You will always miss your child. You realize that your future with your child is no longer possible.

Thinking positively and remembering all the beautiful things about your child will lead you to a healthier outlook on life.

## DEFINITIONS APPLIED TO EMOTIONS OF GRIEF

As you go through the emotions of Grief, you want to understand what you are going through, to understand why Grief controls all of your feelings. For example, when you lose a child, the strength of Grief is something a parent rarely has experienced. It is debilitating to the mind and soul.

As you progress in this long journey, you strive to stay positive. To understand Grief better, I looked over definitions in Webster's dictionary, such as sadness, depression, and anxiety, which seemed to ring true. Then, as I moved forward in my journey, I reviewed positive, uplifting definitions like joy, happiness, and appreciation.

These definitions encompass deep emotions, and you feel vulnerable when you grieve. You hope and pray to feel joy and happiness again someday. As you read this, it may sound odd that I read disheartening and uplifting definitions. For a bereaved parent, normalcy is difficult to achieve, so you search for anything to heal and survive your loss. Bereaved parents are not crazy; we explore all the avenues for some joy after suffering a significant loss.

# EMOTIONS OF GRIEF

These words and definitions are part of a bereaved parent's Grief. The definitions are those stated in Webster's dictionary:

*DISTRESS, SUFFERING, MISERY, and AGONY* mean the state of being in great trouble.
*DISTRESS implies an external and usually temporary cause of significant* physical or mental strain and stress. For example, the death of a loved one puts everyone in great *distress.*
*SUFFERING* implies conscious endurance of pain or distress. There is an element of *suffering during* mental hardship and physical pain.
*MISERY* stresses unhappiness, especially in sickness, poverty, or loss. But unfortunately, the homeless live in *misery* every day.
*AGONY* suggests the pain is so intense over their child's death, it results in unbearable deep and long-lasting pain.

Emotional responses such as anxiety, anguish, anger, crying, denial, depression, despair, emptiness, fatigue, forgetfulness, helplessness, insomnia, irritability, loneliness, mental fog, nightmares, and numbness are normal. In addition, being overwhelmed with regret, sadness, shock, stress, vindictiveness, and worry are just a few of the emotions one goes through.

If you are not a bereaved parent, understand that a parent who has lost a child has gone through a lifetime of emotions in a brief timeframe. Be patient and caring to that person; it is a very fragile situation.

## Joy and Happiness

As one manages through all the Grief, things do get better slowly. Initially, you think getting past all the sadness and loneliness is impossible. However, there is joy and happiness in our lives; sometimes, it takes a significant loss to understand complete pleasure. The true definition of joy goes beyond the limited explanation presented in a dictionary: "a feeling of great pleasure and happiness."

The information on this website describes the difference between joy and happiness.

*Reference https://www.gotquestions.org/joy-happiness.html*

Joy and happiness are often used interchangeably, but there is a big difference between them. Happiness is described as "dependent on external circumstances." The happy feelings are often "like a butterfly that lands on us and then flutters away."

Eating a piece of chocolate or getting all the green lights on the way home from work may make us feel happy for a time, but this satisfaction does not last. Happiness is often associated with feelings of the senses; it is an emotional response.

Joy, on the other hand, *comes from within.* It is a much more enduring feeling that persists no matter the circumstance.

It requires the utmost surrender and, like love, is a choice to be made. Joy is not simply a feeling that happens.

Joy is also not great happiness or even extreme happiness.

It is not elation, jubilation, or exhilaration. But, in its most authentic expression, joy transforms difficult times into blessings and turns heartache into gratitude. Joy brings meaning to life. It brings life to life.

Regardless of faith, joy is present inside everyone as an untapped potential reservoir. It's possible to experience joy in difficult times. Despite the uncertainty, it's possible to feel joy and contentment. Joy doesn't need a smile to exist.

Although joy does feel better with a happy smile, joy can share space with other emotions — sadness, fear, anger, even unhappiness. Happiness can't.

Happiness isn't present in darkness and difficulty. But once discovered, joy undergirds our spirits and brings to life peace and contentment, even in the face of unhappiness.

Joy is present in every moment, and happiness is fleeting and temporary. It's mostly just passing through.

When happiness is present, it's larger than life. It feels good, and nothing feels better or seems worthy of attention. But happiness is also fickle. It can be present for weeks on end and go in an instant. True joy is constant.

In summary, a bereaved parent knows these are just a few primary emotions in Grief. A bereaved parent may experience over 150 common emotions at the death of a loved one. Joy and happiness are goals we all want to achieve to live freely and contentedly. As we go through life, we desire to be safe, happy, and joyful.

# CHAPTER 32

# THE UNSPOKEN TRUTH ABOUT GRIEF

## REFLECTIONS

In the following chapters, I expand on how the death of my child affected me mentally and physically—saying goodbye to your loved one or not being able to say goodbye results in high anxiety. Your search for facts intensifies as you attempt to get answers. There are emotional moments during your Grief when you start questioning your purpose on this earth. Getting through the first year presents significant challenges. You try to help people understand what you are going through. It is best to start caring for yourself because you become drained and exhausted. I share the physical pain and ailments of Grief because it is all-consuming.

People change, and there are variations in people's demeanor. As you assess how you handle your Grief, you realize that you want to live. You do not want to die. However, early on, during the first few months, you want to die to see your child again. You think about your mortality and how your loss has affected your broken heart. As a result, you may become numb to other events or start feeling resentment in the oddest ways. You wear a mask to get through the day and may become fearful of other tragedies because you have no more energy to handle another loss.

You work hard to control these difficult emotions, especially around others or in public. Over time, this becomes less of a challenge, and you learn how to keep control of your feelings during the sorrowful reminders you are bound to have at unexpected times.

## SAYING GOODBYE

Life is sometimes so challenging. When your child dies suddenly, there is no time to say goodbye. So instead, you remember your last moments, your previous conversation, with photographic precision, which is vivid and intensely painful.

You remember when you heard that your child was gone, and it stays with you, and it is the beginning of your world turned upside down. When the shock sets in, your mind goes into an emergency shutdown. You're left helpless and flooded with more than you can handle. Finally, you go numb, and your response is beyond your control. Everything you do emotionally seems to be beyond your control.

There is no timetable to say goodbye. My child's death brought searing pain and initial fleeting thoughts of suicide. The suicidal thoughts are from the shock and trauma, but they subside. Unfortunately, these thoughts are a common occurrence documented many times by parents who have lost their child.

When reality sets in, you realize you had no chance to help stop what happened. No chance to hold your child one more time and say how much you love them and how proud you are of them. Your opportunity to tell your child how important they are in your life is gone. All of this is so sudden and devastating.

It does bring a sense of helplessness and loneliness that creates the saddest emotions and is hard to describe or explain. But eventually you move forward with positive thoughts and start remembering the better moments that will last a lifetime.

## What-ifs

As mentioned previously, a bereaved parent will question the "what-ifs," maybe taking some blame, searching for the facts, and trying to understand why this happened. To expand on these thoughts, these "what-ifs" are intensely painful, and you torment yourself because you feel that you could have done more to prevent the loss of your child. Unfortunately, the "if-only" thoughts never go away. One can expect to live with them forever when you lose a child. It just can't consume you, but you will constantly be questioning what more you could have done.

Sometimes, you expect to have self-blame for the sudden death of a child. There can be guilty feelings about things you have or have not said or done. I wrote this in my birthday letter to Amanda just two months after she died.

You feel helpless because any apology falls on deaf ears, but you pray and hope your child can hear you from heaven. Siblings also sometimes feel this way. My family, my son, and my other daughter felt somewhat guilty about not doing or saying the right things just before Amanda died. This guilt is Grief at its worst. It is the helpless feeling a parent or siblings can feel. We all believed that whatever we didn't do to support Amanda, she would not only forgive, it would not even cross her mind. It was time for our family to endure and stay strong, even among the many emotional meltdowns that occur when you least expect them.

Through reading many books, I have realized that mothers and fathers could lose themselves in endless Grief for years and not endure suffering the right way. Therefore, it is essential to understand all the expectations of Grief.

The more I understood Grief and the arduous journey, the more tolerable life became.

You will forever carry the sadness in your heart for your child. You keep that place in your heart and open yourself back up to the rest of your family and friends. You have to open up your heart, knowing that this journey may take months, maybe much longer, to feel normal again.

## Amanda's gravesite – Emotional moments

Parents who have lost a child have different feelings about their child's gravesite. Some parents cannot bear the thought of visiting their child's grave during the early months after their death. It becomes all too much heartbreak, and it can become impossible to relieve the despair in your heart. Other parents prefer to visit their child's gravesite every day. Going to the cemetery was hard for me, but I wanted to tell my child I loved her. So early on, I would visit every day to be there. Sometimes I did not say a word but just stood there wondering, *Why? Why did God take my child away from me?* As time passes, you learn to accept the reality of it all.

You can become distraught at the idea of your child being just feet away from you. When it rained or was cold or snowed, I would become saddened and anxious at the thought that my child was underground in the wet cold. Even when the sun went down, it upset me that my child was in the dark. Thinking this way sounds unrealistic, but it happens. The things that go through your mind frequently don't make sense. Nothing about the death of your child makes sense.

## QUESTIONING YOUR PURPOSE

Early on, such as in the first few months and sometimes the first couple of years, life becomes a world of emptiness. In my own experience, the void continued beyond the first year. The emptiness and loneliness remain over time; you pray that you can fill that emptiness with some joy and purpose in life without your child. You ask yourself, "Why am I still here, and my child is gone?" My daughter's purpose in life was always to be kind and forgive—not to judge but to offer compassion. She was a caretaker in so many ways. It's an admirable character trait.

So with Grief, especially during the first year, all your feelings intensify. Let me explain. You may be watching a movie, and someone dies, and you start to tear up. You watch acts of kindness on TV or in real life and tear up. You go shopping in a store you were last in with your child, and you tear up. You sit in the car at a red light and see something that reminds you of your child, and you tear up. You look at pictures or post videos of your child; finally, you lose total control of your emotions and mentally and emotionally break down. It feels like insanity, but it is not. You expect these feelings with Grief, especially acute distress, when it is still raw in your mind, and you wonder if it will ever end.

Now you start to believe that there is a purpose for you. You have to continue to move forward. Your child would want you to be happy again. So you become determined to move forward and be kind, support people, and volunteer to help people less fortunate, just as my daughter did.

## GETTING THROUGH THE FIRST YEAR

For your sanity, you have to start to believe the pain will not always be so intense and frequent. You experience many over-whelming moments and try not to lose control at unpredictable times. Each person's pain thresholds are different, and you pray the pain will subside. To get well, you tell yourself that you will not always feel this way. If you don't start believing, you may fal-ter into long-term depression, and you may never be able to live with some joy in your child's memory.

There is a strong need to connect with others who have expe-rienced this unexpected loss. They could relate to the internal mental pain. It may be family members, your spouse or part-ner, a good longtime friend, or someone completely new in your life—maybe a person you meet and become aware that person also has suffered the loss of a child. Over some additional time, when you feel more comfortable and less out of control, it may be time to consider a group to talk about your Grief, such as "Compassionate Friends." This group involves parents who have also lost a child. You ponder these options constantly during Grief.

You will find your true friends, but don't judge those who disap-pear. Every person has a unique way of facing someone who has lost a child. As I mentioned, people generally feel uncomfortable talking with you about your loss. However, other parents who have lost a child can connect with you because they know the actual pain of your loss. People who think they can understand don't know the depth of this type of anguish. People who have lost a child understand as no one else can.

## Help people understand how you feel

Letting people know it is OK to talk about your child is essential. Sharing these thoughts may take some time. You want to keep memories alive for yourself and in other people's minds. You realize that some people will avoid you or avoid the subject of your child's death.

Communication is always the key to helping yourself and others understand Grief. Being open and honest was especially important for me with my other children and spouse, who were also grieving and having difficulty after seeing how death changes family dynamics. Unfortunately, families sometimes go silent and suppress everything. Ignoring the pain of your loss is not a healthy option. Silence is not golden in this case.

It is important to speak up, communicate and nurture your children, regardless of age.

## Taking care of yourself

Grieving alone is something to embrace. In my journey, I was emotional and shed tears most days for 120 days straight. I remember shaking through the night every night for at least 90 continuous days. You think it will never end and doesn't totally end, but you shed tears and shake less often over time. The shaking was shocking to me. Even though the tears never seem to subside, you may not want them to disappear. It sounds crazy, but even though you want the pain to end, you don't mind when the tears continue to show your love for your child. Grieving in private saved me from increased excessive meltdowns. It becomes so important to take care of yourself. I lost weight and looked years older from always being emotional. The aches and pains became physical, and the mental anguish became insurmountable. But as you force yourself to eat well or even start eating, you will gain the calories and strength to bear another day of Grief.

As I have read in many books, you are mentally in an Intensive Care Unit (ICU) during acute Grief. People may expect you to participate in family activities, attend events, or celebrate birthdays or holidays. However, if you were physically in a bad accident, laid up, and unable to get out of bed, people would not expect you to participate in these activities.

So you treat yourself well and learn to say no. You decide to stay true to your Grief. You may have zero energy, and socializing is challenging, even with family, and it can be draining. It's not your fault that you feel this way. It is normal during these difficult times. Thinking of surviving each day becomes your new normal.

## DRAINED AND EXHAUSTED

You move forward to take care of yourself but are still drained and exhausted. All your energy goes toward making it through those emotional days that do not seem to end. You cannot always help other people or participate in those family activities. Your pain is so intense the first few months that it disables you. It isn't easy to get up in the morning and go through the motions each day. You start feeling like a zombie. It was vital for me to push back and make myself a priority.

There will be times when you have nothing to give. You may feel weak and inadequate. Actually, you are inadequate when you suffer a tremendous loss that results in unimaginable mental pain. You are in that mental ICU, and no one can dispute that you are inadequate.

However, there is something inside a bereaved person's heart. Because you have felt the pain of losing a child, you ignite human emotions rarely felt by someone who has not suffered a significant loss. You will become more compassionate than ever because you have lived through a loss not experienced by others. Your senses are now in full gear.

# CHAPTER 33

# PHYSICAL PAIN AND AILMENTS

RESEARCH STUDIES INDICATE that there is physical pain during acute Grief, especially during the first 4-6 months. My physical pain included chest pressure, shortness of breath, high blood pressure from the stress, aches and muscle pain, back pain, stomach issues, dizziness, and extreme shaking. You are on an emotional rollercoaster so expect the unexpected.

There is unpredictability, and you may feel out of control. There will be times when you think you are going crazy. It is normal to be blindsided by emotions as you are grieving.

Stress brings on physical ailments and depletes your immune system. Studies have shown that the immune system of parents who lose a child unexpectedly showed significant alterations in biochemically measurable components. Even after many months, these biological components in your body remain altered. So the Grief of unexpectedly losing a child changes your biological makeup due to extreme stress. Over time, by doing all the right things to get well, your body will heal, and your immune system will strengthen, but it may never be as strong as before your child's death. You are a changed person, both emotionally and physically. For me, the tragic loss of my daughter created significant mental and physical challenges. It's best to move forward with positive thoughts, take care of your health, have compassion for others, and finally try to accept the unacceptable loss.

## PHYSICAL IMPACTS OF GRIEF

You have apparent physical impacts when you grieve for your lost child. You look different, and you feel different—a story to tell.

I joined a fitness center about a month into my Grief. On my first visit, I explored the exercise classes and observed the different types of exercise equipment. It was four months since Amanda died, and I wanted to regain some sense of fitness. Before Amanda died, I enjoyed a full schedule of fitness activities every week. These activities included playing tennis and golf twice a week, and working out at the fitness center twice a week. After four months, I decided to work out for the first time. Previously, I used between 50 and 70 pounds of weight on various types of exercise equipment and was able to complete 100 sit-ups regularly. This time it was different. I had lost my strength. I was limited to 20 pounds on the equipment and finished about 20 sit-ups. My point here is that this is what grieving can do to you. It mentally drains you and can sap the strength out of your body. I was going through the motions during the first four months.

## GRIEF CAUSES CLUMSINESS

During the first year of Grief, several puzzling clumsiness instances occurred. I experienced bumping into walls, tripping while walking, or becoming unbalanced at various times. I played tennis most of my life and enjoyed the exercise. It was a way to stay active during my Grief. However, I fell or tripped so often that I had severe bruises on my backside, shoulder, hands, and arms. Then I read stories about how clumsiness is typical when grieving. People in Grief reported falling, breaking their leg, or falling down the stairs.

So it all started to make sense. Being clumsy may surprise you, but it happens, and Grief affects everything, physically and mentally. It makes you pause, and you move more carefully throughout the day. Of course, one thinks that clumsiness can also be part of aging. You may observe a change in your balance caused mainly by dizziness or your mind just being in a fog.

## GRIEF IS ALL-CONSUMING

Taking care of your body and getting some exercise is essential, even if it's just taking a walk outside to clear your mind. You need to give yourself a break from the Grief.

I experienced prolonged Grief during my difficult journey and let all my emotions out. However, there comes a time when you must decide to dig yourself out of this prolonged, complicated Grief. Nothing comes easy as you go through the motions, and you may realize that it feels good to release the stress and tension by just taking that walk outside.

I enjoyed looking up to the sky to feel the sun and see some brightness. Appreciating nature helped me. It sounds absurd, but it is the truth.

Grief is so all-consuming that it is normal to feel out of control. Being disoriented, confused, in a fog, and somewhat forgetful is normal in despair, especially acute distress during the first several months and maybe the first year. As mentioned, bumping into furniture, dropping things, and sometimes being unbalanced were regular occurrences. Likewise, memory loss and forgetfulness were common occurrences.

As I read more books about Grief and losing a child, there were stories and opinions that the second year might be more complex than the first year. Many bereaved parents have more difficulty accepting their child's death when they realize they must learn to live without their child.

This realization sent me into a sad state of mind. Maybe I was reading too much in the early months, and sometimes too much information can set you back. But how can anything be worse in the second year than what you go through during the first year? I reached my second year, but I know the first year was undeniably the most challenging. The longing feelings and missing your loved one may be constant, and you melt from the stress of the Grief. A parent who loses a child is usually exhausted most of the time.

It becomes a cycle of tiredness. However, you must think and avoid spiraling down a black hole you can never escape.

## GRIEF LASTS FOREVER

*Quote by Elizabeth Kubler-Ross and David Kessler: "The ... - Goodreads. https://www.goodreads.com/quotes/442107-the-reality-is-that-you-will-grieve-forever.*

*The reality is that you will grieve forever. You will not "get over" the loss of your child; you will learn to live with it. You will heal and will rebuild yourself around the loss you have suffered. You will be whole again but never be the same, nor would you want to.*

## Grief is a walk alone.

*Quote by Cathy Lamb: "But Grief is a walk alone. Others ... - Goodreads. https://www.goodreads.com/quotes/545914-but-Grief-is-a-walk-alone.*

*It is a lonely time in your life. Others can be there and listen. But you will walk alone down your own path, at your own pace, with your sheared-off pain, raw wounds, broken heart, denial, guilt, and bitter loss. You will come to your own peace, hopefully...but you will be on your own, hopefully...but it will be **on your own, in your own time, in your own way.***

# CHAPTER 34

# ASSESSING HOW YOU ARE DOING

IT IS ESSENTIAL to continue assessing how you are doing and understand if you are progressing. Some triggers set off your emotions when you think you are doing well. For example, the clock we received at Christmas from my stepdaughter and husband would play a particular tune on the hour. When the clock chimed on this early morning hour and played that Christmas song, "What Child is this," it reminded me of the Christmas holiday spent without my daughter.

These are triggers that will stop you cold in your recovery from Grief. When you think you are making progress, there will be setbacks. It's important to remember that you are still making progress. Setbacks are common and expected. Nevertheless, you strive to move forward with the determination that there can be some happiness and joy in your life.

## EMERGING FROM SUICIDAL THOUGHTS TO WANTING TO LIVE

Early on, there are those terrible feelings and thoughts of suicide. Fortunately, they do pass, and counseling professionals have documented that most parents have initial ideas about suicide when they suffer this kind of tremendous loss in their lives. It is a normal thought as long as it is not consuming. If it doesn't pass, experts advise that it is imperative to seek out a medical professional to help you get past these thoughts. You may not feel that you will act on these thoughts, but you may still think this way for a short while. Then, especially during the first few months, you may feel, as I did in my journey, that you don't want to die but don't want to live. There is a difference. Wanting to live in the early stages of your Grief seems impossible.

You are disabled in your mind and do not have any feelings or energy to move forward.

You want your child back, and you want to hold and talk to your child just once more. There will come a time when you do want to live and you do want to move forward. It's healthy to embrace your personal timeline and take your time based on your state of mind. It is best not to let others push your timeline. Stand firm and do what you feel is most important to you. If you rush it or suppress the emotions, it will extend your suffering.

You will wonder daily when the pain will end. So privately grieve if you must, but feel free to grieve whenever necessary.

In time, you will want to live.

## YOUR HEART IS YOUR CASTLE

Within one's heart, there are many emotions, including extreme love and affection for your spouse, children, family members, friends, partners, and relatives.

Each member of your family is so passionately vital to you. You go through life with your heart filled with compassion for your family. My family is large by traditional standards, and they are wonderful. However, not all families share loving continuity and understanding for each other. As life goes on and you lose a part of your family, the intensity of the loss sometimes depends on your relationship with that family member.

Losing your wife or partner may result in severe loss, especially if your relationship is solid and years-long—the bond with your biological children is undeniably the strongest. You would die for your children or trade places in a minute if it meant that it would save your child's life. For many parents, this is indeed true.

So when you experience a death in your extended family, like an uncle or cousin, you grieve; it affects you significantly. But it subsides, and life goes on; you can function normally with a memory that stays with you.

With the loss of your parents, there is extreme sadness. When your first parent dies, you are usually in shock and denial, and the Grief is intense.

It may last several months, but you realize that your mother or father lived a long life, and you rationalize that they are now in a better place. The hole in your heart now begins to shrink. When your second parent dies, there is a more traumatic effect, and you are a bit lost and grieve harder and longer because now both of your parents are gone. Now maybe you feel that you are an orphan. If you were close to your parents in your upbringing, now you suddenly have no one to support you. You may realize all the good things your parents did for you. But your heart heals over time.

In these instances, you are temporarily heartbroken. You have those memories, and the shadow stays with you in the memories you hold. It is somewhat of an unspoken rule that your most substantial love and affection are for your immediate biological family and your spouse. You nurture these relationships for many years, and losing close family members causes significant Grief. The trauma of losing a spouse would be undeniably awful and crushing. When a spouse passes within a relatively short period after their partner's death, some believe they die of a broken heart. Sometimes the loneliness and sadness and the lack of a will to live without your partner become too much to bear.

The loss of a child is like the amputation of part of your heart. It doesn't grow back. The loss is significant because you feel that part of you has died. Your child, whom you have raised and protected all those years, is gone. The future with your child is gone. Your relationship is gone. It is almost impossible to accept. It is excruciating to grieve the loss of a child. In the early stages of grieving, you feel that you can never be happy again.

You attempt to start turning the tragedy of losing your child into positive memories. Then, hopefully, the deep hole in your heart starts to heal, and you still have a heartbeat. First, however, you must continue living with your child's memories. You will always have your child in your memory. Everyone around you will live on, and you know inside of you is a broken heart that you must accept, but you will never forget your loving child. You can't, and you won't because you know that if you ever forget your child's love, you will die inside.

It becomes almost unbearable when your child dies before you. It creates a whole new set of challenges in your Grief. When your child dies, you feel that part of you dies also, but you know that your family needs you, and you pray for strength to recover and heal. Believe as I did that God has His plan. He suffered and died for us, and God has also experienced Grief. If you are a non-believer, you should understand that you will see your child again.

It helped me immensely, and these thoughts allowed me to survive my loss.

# CHAPTER 35

# RESENTMENT, NUMBNESS, AND FEAR

WHEN YOU GRIEVE, sometimes you come across what you think is the perfect family. There was resentment and envy when I saw what appeared to be the ideal family. I questioned why God gave them the joy of having all their children healthy and seeing their lives flourish. When you know of a family that has suffered no loss, not a parent's death or a child's tragedy, you wonder why this happened to you. Why has God given you the broken pieces of your life while sparing others? We will never know why. I trusted that this was God's plan. If we don't believe, the world will crumble around us. How can a parent feel your pain when they have not experienced a child's death? It is impossible. They can only imagine, but the reality is that the pain is much greater than they could imagine.

No one is at fault.

The perfect family does not exist, but in reality, death will come in some form over a family's lifetime. It is inevitable, and it is the truth. Unfortunately, we do not always know what hardships a family has experienced. Over a lifetime, no ideal family is free from distress or despair. Realizing this helped me bear the weight of losing my child.

## BECOMING FEARFUL ABOUT ANOTHER TRAGEDY

There is a fear that you cannot handle another tragedy when you have experienced losing a child. You don't have the resilience or emotional strength to manage another tragedy. When you think about it, there are so many dramatic, heartbreaking stories of parents learning that their loved ones have died. Many parents have lost multiple children, sometimes drastically all at once, maybe in a car accident. Think about it for just a moment. Can you imagine a mother or father hearing that a tragic car accident killed all their children and spouse? Unfortunately, tragic events happen in our lives.

I read a story about a wife who gave her husband a birthday present: a ride in a hot-air balloon with his best friend. As the balloon lifted her husband and his best friend into the sky, she followed him in her car to enjoy the experience. Suddenly, the hot-air balloon malfunctioned and started dropping from the sky. The wife tragically watched her husband and his best friend fall to their death. It was his birthday present that ended in tragedy.

Many parents have suffered through losing their child or children in a violent death. Some children disappear, never to be found again. It is difficult to imagine knowing your child has died and there is no trace of where they are. Unfortunately, so many children in our country have disappeared from horrible acts of human trafficking or kidnapping. It is inconceivable to envision these tragic events.

These stories make one realize that others have also experienced significant tragedies. A loss is a loss. When you lose a loved one, there is an immediate fear of another tragedy. Life holds no guarantees. You can't compare tragedies because your tragedy feels like the worst thing that has happened to you. But others may suffer significant losses, and you might not even be aware. Therefore you live your life with more compassion toward others, because you never know the pain they may be experiencing.

# CHAPTER 36

# MY ROAD TO SURVIVAL

## INTRODUCTION

When one is experiencing extended or unresolved Grief, the recovery takes a long time to manage and becomes a lonely road. It is like the book's title, *A Road Less Traveled*. You do not wish trauma on anyone. There are many decisions that you have to make. First, you realize that your life has become a new normal. Culture and expectations of your Grief will create some stress. The road to my survival involved participating in activities that began relieving stress. Next, you have to make decisions on counseling and medication. Finding quiet time and solitude is critical as you try to recover from the stress. You must keep your child active in your memory, find peace through appreciation, and realize your blessings. Finally, your search for faith leads you to believe there is a special place when you die—where you will see your child again.

## A MAN'S DILEMMA WITH GRIEF – CULTURE AND EXPECTATIONS

The book *Men are from Mars, Women are from Venus* is about how different men are from women when showing emotions and how we communicate. Men have little to talk about with male friends, and the subjects usually include sports, travel, or maybe their favorite steak restaurants.

My point is that men don't open up very quickly about personal feelings. On the other hand, women can talk at length about their feelings, put their emotions on their sleeves, and discuss unique things about their lives very easily with their friends. So when it comes to grieving, men are usually less emotional than women.

Maybe I was different, but many men relent to the weight of emotions when dealing with the loss of their child. The "so-called" strongest men who have never cried for as long as they can remember will fall apart and feel a weakness they never experienced before.

Some men are Marines, police chiefs, Army Special Forces, doctors, and lawyers or strong-willed men, will fall apart and sob uncontrollably at the death of their child.

Grief will bring tears. Suffering is more potent than one can imagine, bringing one to their knees in indescribable pain.

I felt an internal pride in being emotional about family and passionate about protecting my children over the years. Some say it takes great courage and strength to let your emotions flow. Others may privately see you as weak. You may see a change in how people treat you over the months and years ahead; you know you are a changed person. You anticipate that your Grief will be long and difficult moving forward.

It is essential to forge ahead, make new friends who can understand Grief, and be aware of friends who do not understand your pain. You may hear many adverse reactions from people even though they unintentionally hurt you. "It's time to get over it already," "It's time to move on," or "When are you going to get on with your life?"

Fortunately, my family and friends have not said these things, but it does happen. If your friends or family speak like this, I would not think they understand compassion. Understand that sometimes people don't realize that their words may hurt more than they help. When you grieve, you must move ahead with compassion and understanding. If you decide to part with some friends, it is not judging; it is protecting yourself.

## SHADOW GRIEF – OUR NEW NORMAL

Sometimes you may feel that you are a stranger trapped inside your body. You will wonder if you will ever find contentment again. Instead, you will search for happiness, tranquility, and serenity.

Eventually, you reach a place where your everyday existence is not painful to the point where you are always emotional. You realize the sharp pains and emotions start to dull as time passes.

Your tears that seemed never to stop will start to recede, and you will begin to live in the shadows. I have read that this is what grievers call "Shadow Grief." As you experience every morning, every night, and as you attend family outings, birthdays, holidays, and anniversaries, you are living in a shadow; this is normal for bereaved parents.

You live with a permanent sadness that engulfs your heart. You are now a shadow of the person you once were. But this is what you desire. You will feel that this is how you have to live your life.

You will learn to enjoy many things moving forward, but it will take time. You embrace the shadow. The shadow is your heartfelt memories of your child. How could you not move forward without your child's shadow always in your heart? You will be determined never to forget your child; keeping these memories within you will lead you to live everyday life; this will be your new normal. You are now living in a new era. Your new world will be livable, and you may realize that you have other family members, children, and friends with whom you can learn to live a life filled of joy and happiness along with your shadow child.

## GROUP THERAPY OR PROFESSIONAL COUNSELING

The decision to attend group or professional counseling is up to each individual; we are all different. Professional counselors have documented that group counseling can be very harmful. In group counseling, a bereaved parent can grieve for years and hold onto memories that distract them from fully healing from their loss. However, on a positive note, some grieving parents embrace group therapy and meet others to connect with and become lifetime friends.

Therefore, group counseling was an avenue I strongly considered. I wondered if I would be the only man in group counseling such as "Compassionate Friends." During the first year of my journey, with my private personality, I felt more comfortable grieving alone. You know, in group counseling, you will hear heartbreaking stories. Every loss is tragic, and no single one is more painful than another. You can't compare tragedies. I thought hearing these stories would set me back. Whether it is an expected or sudden, unexpected loss, it is still a heartbreaking loss.

I read stories that professional counseling sometimes doesn't work. It depends on several things. One, did the professional counselor experience the loss of a child? If not, you tend not to believe or take that counselor seriously because you know there is no way they can feel the actual searing pain you have experienced. Second, there has to be a proper connection for you. Finally, whether it is a man or woman counselor, you must have the trust and feeling that you can discuss anything without embarrassment.

Some counselors advise you, try to fix you, and make you feel better. Some counselors listen and accept that grieving parents need someone to listen to and be comforted. It will be your decision. Finding the right person or outlet is essential if a particular counselor or group counseling doesn't initially work. As for me, I was patient in my grieving timeline. There was little urgency to receive different kinds of help immediately. My private grieving was my chosen path to healing. However, looking back on the past year, it would have been helpful to learn the techniques and advice provided by a professional to resolve acute grieving.

## MEDICATION OR NO MEDICATION

There are differing opinions on whether or not to medicate for grieving, anxiety, and depression. However, an anti-depressant can be beneficial. It provides energy, reduces stress, makes you think clearly, and helps you sleep. Initially, I started taking medication only for a short time because I didn't believe it was doing me any good. Earlier in my Grief, I felt no medicine could mask the shock, trauma, and despair of losing my child. So I discontinued taking an anti-depressant. However, I will reconsider if it's difficult to regain energy and sleep better at night. After many months, the sleepless nights became less frequent, and my sleep hours increased during the second half of the first year.

Some professionals state that taking an anti-depressant numbs your feelings and doesn't help you experience the full effects of Grief. It only delays the process and extends your grieving period. It is not possible to know how long the grieving will last. You hope the intense moments and waves of Grief will subside to a more manageable level. You have to decide what is best for you. Medication may be worth a try if you experience prolonged, extended periods of sadness and extended, debilitating periods of sorrow. You see, there are always two sides to the story.

## FINDING NEW ACQUAINTANCES WHO LOST A CHILD

I know two couples who tragically lost their children. One lost their four-month-old daughter from SIDs, and the other lost their son in a violent act of murder. Yet, these special people helped me understand what to expect moving forward. I will never forget their kindness and compassion.

Being patient with yourself while grieving has its benefits. So there was no rush to search for that someone with whom I could be comfortable discussing my Grief. Instead, it was my choice to grieve privately. In time, I will find others who lost their child unexpectedly. There will be a common bond and understanding in sharing our loss. So if you want to reach out to someone or attend a Grief counseling group, I recommend doing this at your own pace and on your timeline. We all know that help is available, and each person must determine the best way forward.

## SILENT NIGHTS – 20 MINUTES OF THOUGHT

You realize that with time, you will start feeling better. Your desire to get relief from the helplessness is overwhelming. You are skeptical about reaching that plateau of feeling normal during those early months. Thoughts of your loved one are all-consuming almost every day. Sometimes you are distracted from sad thoughts by staying busy exercising, engaging in activities, doing chores, shopping, or working on a project. After months of Grief, I found peace by spending 20 minutes of private time thinking about my daughter every evening before falling asleep. You think about all the beautiful times and remember clear images of when you shared memorable moments. When I visited Amanda's apartment, she proudly told me how clean she kept the apartment and was proud of her stocked refrigerator filled with healthy food. She was excited to exercise at the gym while her mother babysat little Ellie. Amanda received food stamps and was so grateful to use these to buy Ellie the food she needed.

So I reminisced about all the things Amanda appreciated but still wondered why she needed to take an antidepressant to a level that ended her life. Maybe she experienced another panic attack worrying about family matters. Perhaps she wasn't aware of the danger. You try to stay positive in your thoughts, but it can be a grueling effort to do so. The 20 minutes helped me remember the wonderful times shared with Amanda, even if this quiet time of reflection caused more tears to flow. So into my second year of Grief, I still set aside 20 minutes every night to reflect on the positive accomplishments in her life. I recommend that any bereaved parent take some time during each day, not necessarily before bed; this time may work for you, but may cause others a more restless night.

## Daily Morning prayers and emotions

Nighttime was the best time to reflect on the beautiful memories of my daughter. It's a time of peacefulness and solitude. Mornings may bring loneliness and hollow feelings of emptiness because you wake up and initially think your child is still with you. Then you are fully awake and feel distraught in an instant. You pray that your loved one is safe and content. It was healthy for me to stay in a daily routine. Daily prayers were part of my routine. I would make a pot of coffee, sit at the computer, and continue to write in a journal, which I have transformed into this book.

I wanted this book to be part of my salvation, my legacy, to tell the world how Grief changes your life. It's important for people reading this book to see a possible way to heal during the most trying time a parent can endure. This book will be for Amanda, so she can see that her death revealed a mountain of love for her in our family. These thoughts are typical for a bereaved parent— at least, that is what I believe.

Writing this book was the best way to manage the days of excru-ciating Grief. As you reflect on all the life events of your loved one, the Grief can consume you. Yet you do everything in your power to get well and make it through this journey. Writing this book became less painful as the months passed, and it provided a critical outlet for me to exhaust all the feelings and effects of grieving for my lost child.

# CHAPTER 37

# SPIRITUAL BELIEFS

I WAS RAISED Catholic and attended church every Sunday. As a young boy, I would go to confession every month to confess my sins and would write my sins on paper to remember them for the month. After acknowledging my sins to the priest, I remember feeling free, excited with pure energy as I left the confession box. In those days, telling a fib or saying a bad word were sins on my list.

Reflecting on these moments, you realize these innocent sins were no comparison to the sins committed in today's world, where violence is prevalent across the country.

As a young boy, I found the Bible confusing, as it most likely is for all children at an early age. Most people have their thoughts and beliefs. With all the cultures and religions around the world, faith is all the same. In different religions, most people believe in an afterlife, God, or a higher being. Some don't think so, but the day will come when we will all see and experience the truth.

I sat in disbelief at my daughter's grave for many weeks. After that, my faith wavered, and I didn't trust God. How could He have taken my child when she loved God, cherishing and singing to him every day and night? My daughter loved God and always said that God has His plan, and when she was having a difficult day, she would tell me that she would leave it to God and everything would be fine.

Over time, my beliefs changed, and I began to trust God. Not everyone believes, and that is understandable. Believing in an afterlife was the only way to envision seeing my child again. That is your hope, and your journey begins with finding genuine faith, not just asking for forgiveness from a list of sins you put on a piece of paper when you were a child.

A bereaved parent wonders why their child died, and they are still alive. You wish to trade places with your deceased child. It is not the correct order of life. We never expect to outlive our children. It is a raw, emotional experience that debilitates one's mind. Reading some books on Near Death Experiences (NDEs) and heaven helped me tremendously, which provided hope and faith. Heaven was a focus of mine during this time. When you are heartbroken, you reach for a more decisive way to manage the Grief, trauma, and despair.

## IMAGINING HEAVEN AND BELIEVING IN GOD

There are intriguing books on heaven and Near Death Experiences. The books titled *Imagine Heaven*, *90 days in Heaven*, and *Life after Life* share many stories of people seeing what they think is Heaven, only to come back to their earthly bodies. The best of them, *Imagine Heaven*, details hundreds of Near Death Experiences, God's promises, and the exhilarating future that awaits you. It is astonishing that 100 percent of people who have died and experienced a third-dimensional Heaven returned to life and have become Christians.

Even atheists who have not believed in God have turned to God and now believe in the Holy Spirit. They genuinely believe that there is life after death. It has changed their lives. These people have flat-lined—no heartbeat, and no brain activity. These are not only coma victims. People have come back to live here on earth with a new purpose. How could it not change a person's life? Every human being on this planet wonders if there is life after death. When you lose a child, you want to believe that you will see your child in Heaven again someday.

So now you have become dedicated to being a better Christian. Of course, bereaved parents desire to see their loved ones, especially their children, again someday. One wants to feel the happiness, healthiness, and pure joy that Heaven brings to us. Thousands of people experience the light and extreme delight in the place we call Heaven when they leave their earthly bodies, only to return with their stories and experiences.

So I genuinely do not fear death and am not afraid to die. However, after you grieve for long periods, over months, and sometimes years, you desire to live with compassion toward others and be kind to everyone, no matter what they have done or how they have treated you in the past.

You think about how you have changed when you have an enormous loss in your life. But if you truly believe, our time on this earth is temporary, only decided by God, and we have no control over when our time on earth will end. So you learn to appreciate each day God gives you.

*Reference https://www.dreamstime.com/
photos-images/stairway-heaven.html*

# Finding Peace: Searching
## for faith and solitude
# National Shrine Grotto of Lourdes

It was a bitterly cold day in February; the temperature was about eight degrees. Nevertheless, I wanted to gain strength toward more faith and prayer. So I decided to visit the National Shrine Grotto of Lourdes.

*Reference the definition section of this content in National Shrine Grotto - Home. https://www.nsgrotto.org/*

The National Shrine Grotto of Our Lady of Lourdes is a Catholic place of prayer devoted to the Blessed Mother, Mary. This beautiful mountainside shrine features one of the oldest American replicas of the Lourdes Grotto in France, built about two decades after the apparition of Mary at Lourdes in 1858.

Each year, the National Shrine Grotto draws thousands of visitors from all over the world. It is a place of worship, pilgrimage, conversion, and reconciliation.

The Grotto Water taps, located around a fountain pool, have been blessed by priests and, most recently, by Most Reverend William E. Lori, Archbishop of the Archdiocese of Baltimore. This water, offered at the National Shrine Grotto, reminds you of Jesus, who is life-giving water.

The Grotto Chaplain was sometimes available to bless and sanctify the Grotto Water. Once the Grotto Water becomes holy, you can use it to bless persons and places or protect against evil and danger.

Many people visit just for the Grotto Water. Some believe it's cleansing and healthy for the body and soul; others think it can heal. Although no documented miracles exist, many have reported favors and graces from drinking the Grotto Water.

The Grotto is a place of peace and tranquility. It was a short drive from my home, and I visited there many times to grieve my parents' deaths over 20 years ago. It was the place I decided to revisit to help me pray and gain the strength needed to survive each day and remember my daughter. I visited there for the holy water. It was a place for necessary peacefulness and solitude. Finding a place of solitude helps to heal your heart and gain strength to move forward.

# CHAPTER 38

# LEARNING ABOUT APPRECIATION

## APPRECIATION GROWS EXPONENTIALLY

As a grieving parent, one slowly begins to recover from the shock and trauma of losing their child. But you initially feel you can never return to the happy, appreciative person you were before your child's death. This excerpt defines a grieving parent's feelings and resonates with many who have lost a child.

*Reference ABedForMyHeart.com, Author unknown.*

The sun may never shine as brightly as it did before. The full moon may not appear as brilliant as it did before. Flowers, gardens, and art may not look as colorful as they once did. This is the shadow of your child that has put a slight haze over your outlook on life. Some day you will wake up and begin a new journey in your life. You will start to have your senses restored, and your vision will sharpen. But it won't be easy, and it will take time. You realize that you have plenty of time remaining in your life. You will eventually have a stronger desire to enjoy and appreciate the things in life you experienced before your child died. You know that you will have to work hard at this. You will realize that even if you see it as impossible, you must reach out to a trusted friend, doctor, or Grief group. You may reach toward your faith and pray every day if that is what you feel is necessary to get through each day to survive the sadness.

This is the truth about Grief. There are many thoughts and emotions, and it takes time to heal. You start to make the turn by realizing that your new life will be different without your child, but you know your child would not want you to be sad. So you continue to live believing you will see each other again.

You begin to change your perspective to live your life, try to enjoy the small things, and appreciate all the kind people in this world. When troubled, you need to embrace this mindset. Some part of you dies when you lose a child, and you will always carry some sadness. But you realize that this shadow of Grief is your new world.

## MY POCKET GRATITUDE: CHANGED
### MY OUTLOOK ON LIFE

When we learned of my daughter's death, my wife and I boarded a plane and flew from Maryland to South Carolina the next day. We met my former wife, Amanda's mom, at the airport. She was in an apparent broken state of mind, as we all were just one day after discovering my daughter lying on her apartment floor. We drove to Amanda's apartment and fell apart emotionally as we walked in.

It was demoralizing and felt like we were gut-punched and knocked silly and dazed beyond our control. It was another excruciating moment for everyone.

After spending the night in Amanda's bed, it would be my last time visiting her apartment. The feeling is impossible to put into words. It was like a train hit you head-on, and you felt helpless and disoriented. It became a delusional nightmare for us.

As we collected Amanda's personal belongings, we gathered some of the clothes she wore and some books she read daily. I wanted to get into her state of mind because, at that point, we did not know what had happened. She collapsed and died on her floor, and as we learned later, she was probably lying there for 12-16 hours as her three-year-old baby daughter sat on the couch with the television turned on and in a diaper full of sadness. The heartbreak was unbearable at the time we were there.

I gathered Amanda's reading materials, she had multiple Bibles, a journal notebook, and books she read on health and wellbeing. It took me months to look at the material. I reviewed all the notes in Amanda's journal and observed how many sentences and paragraphs were underlined or highlighted in the Bible. Amanda became a strong Christian, but I didn't realize how much she dedicated herself to her faith. Amanda's detailed notes in her journal and the Bible surprised me; she kept several versions.

I reviewed another book by her bed titled *My Pocket Gratitude* by Courtney E. Ackerman.

After four months of having it sit in a drawer, I started to read it. The book indicated all the essential small things that bring you contentment. Amanda always wanted to remain calm. She appreciated all the little things that many of us sometimes take for granted. The book provided many exercises and thoughts on how to live a happy life. The book's back cover read:

> As you go about your day, it's essential to take a moment to appreciate the good things in life. This book lets you

practice gratitude with your mind, body, and spirit. Gratitude transforms any negative situation by adding a positive perspective and makes otherwise ordinary moments joyful. Be grateful for the moments in your life, whether big or small.

As a bereaved parent, you feel more gratitude for what you have. It is not the material things that matter anymore. Compassion and love for family and friends matter most.

There are regrets in life, and you may reflect on the additional times you could have helped your child. Regrets are one of the hardships people may experience, where some guilt may arise. But, as described in this book, you can only forgive yourself and be grateful for all the good things you did to support and protect your child.

As previously mentioned, Amanda was medically diagnosed with anxiety issues, especially social anxiety. However, she grew more outgoing over the last two years, gaining confidence, and succeeded in many ways. This book beside her bed showed me how she wanted to feel normal in a crowd or even at family gatherings.

Amanda would go missing at family gatherings in the past, and we would wonder where she disappeared. I later learned that her social anxiety became overwhelming, and she wanted to be alone for a while to calm down. I did not understand it at the time but learned afterward that this condition could be debilitating, which made my heart sink. It was upsetting when Amanda would disappear for a while. As I reflected on many things, there are regrets for events you wish you could reverse.

# CHAPTER 39

# THE FUTURE – FINDING COMPASSION

## INTRODUCTION

There is hope even when you feel lost, disoriented, and saddened. You will continue to heal over time and wonder what is in the future. I share how I changed, and how my compassion for people became more apparent. You do not fully recover, but you survive and heal differently. You learn to live with some anxiety, and you will go through many months of sleepless nights until complete exhaustion consumes you. But you will begin searching for happiness one moment at a time. You will learn to take nothing for granted. I share my experiences in the hope that you will see that healing is possible.

## HEALING AFTER THE SUDDEN DEATH OF YOUR CHILD

The scars are there that will never go away. You carry a burden with you wherever you go. You will always have a partially broken heart. Yet, you know you have the rest of your life to live.

So what do you do? I asked myself that question many times. *What do I do now? How am I going to be happy again?* You know you have changed in ways you can't even describe. It takes time to heal the wound in your heart. It is all on your own time.

There will come a time when you have to find the hope and strength to continue your life.

Just as you think it will be impossible to be happy again without your child, the days will become brighter, and you will start to think of the good things about your child. I started thinking about all the beautiful memories Amanda brought into my life. The sadness will turn into warm feelings as you think about all the good times you spent with your child. The healing continues. Trust me on this. You might not feel that you can heal, but your child would want to see you healed and knows how much you love them. They see your pain, but you can turn to your faith, look up to the sky, and hold your arms out to your child. You are now on the journey that will give your child peace. You have to believe there is peace in heaven and your future.

## WHAT DOES THE FUTURE LOOK LIKE?

You realize now that you are a bereaved parent and have a future that may seem cloudy to you. You wonder what your future will be like a year from when your child dies. What will my life be like five years from this day moving forward? You will wonder what your purpose is in life.

Why am I here? You may ask yourself that question many times. I began thinking about everything and everyone important in my life. It wasn't material things.

My thoughts turned toward the rest of my family. I began to realize that even though there may be health issues, we have been fortunate and healthy enough to live without traumatic physical injuries. However, some unfortunate people do not have sight or hearing. Many people have lost their ability to think or walk; others are suffering greatly daily with physical and mental challenges. We don't always know what the future holds but realize you have your family and friends. You think about restarting your future with your lost child in your heart and moving forward, living your life with your child's compassion and kindness.

## How you change as a person

I was a different person as soon as I heard my child died. In the beginning, you feel bewildered and lost. You think you have gone through all the emotions imaginable. You attempt to get through all the exhaustion and anxiety. It takes a long time. You have traveled through hell and back, and now you look at yourself as different. So how do you change? I looked at all the emotional wreckage I experienced and tried everything to get well, to get through unimaginable Grief. All those meltdowns and thoughts of going somewhere to heal happened when I was in a fog. So you stand alone and look at yourself. The hope is that you have become resilient to the little things that don't matter.

Sometimes you will see people upset or angry about silly things, and you think, *If they only knew what real pain and real loss felt like, they would not allow ridiculous things to bother them.*

Your emotions become highly magnified. You will feel more empathy. You will cry more at things or events you have never experienced. In a way, you are now more of a whole person, for you have experienced the most significant loss a human being can endure. You lost your child, and no one can understand that pain unless they experience it. You will eventually find people who also have lost a child, and your connection will be solid and real.

You have changed for the better in many ways, and you carry on with your heavy heart for your child's love. Yet you have the passion and resilience to move forward and appreciate all you have.

## FINDING COMPASSION

## A SAD STORY ABOUT TOM

I worked at a golf course as a player's assistant. The job was to drive around the golf course, provide water and towels to the players, and ensure everyone was moving well at their pace to play through the golf course.

My friend Tom was an older gentleman in his 80s. He was a wonderful man and had some physical disabilities. One day after work, he invited me over to his home. His hobby was making wine stoppers with a golf ball attached to the top. It was quite a popular item for golfers and a good gift. He had a contract with the golf clubs in the area to sell these wine stoppers in their golf shops.

He gave me a tour of his home. As I walked through it, I noticed it was in disarray. Tom was alone with his pet dog, and that dog meant everything to him.

Tom showed me pictures of his wife, who had passed a few years ago. Then Tom showed me a book he published about all his memories of himself and his wife. I asked for a copy, and he was glad to share it. His book was beautiful. It was a book of poems about him and his wife and all the memories they had experienced since they were married.

Tom would go to work at the golf course as a player assistant, riding around doing his job. Sometimes Tom would disappear from the golf course. His home was within walking distance of the golf course. Some other employees would joke about Tom disappearing from the golf course and wonder what he was doing.

As I was in his home, Tom showed me his hobby and explained that this kept him busy. He quietly mentioned that he was very lonely, and all he had was his dog and the memories of his loving wife. Tom would leave the golf course during his lunchtime to go home and be with his dog, and he felt the need to comfort himself with memories of his wife while hugging his precious dog. This routine continued for a couple of years. He still grieved his wife after so much time had passed. Tom told me his health was not good, and he was looking forward to reuniting with his wife.

I left his home that day and felt extreme sadness for Tom. Unfortunately, I never circled back to see how he was doing. I did not give him compassion, comfort, or companionship following that day. After losing my precious daughter, I realized how much more I could have done to be a special friend to Tom. Having regrets in life is expected when you lose someone you love. I would have done things very differently after experiencing the pain and suffering of losing my daughter. Anyone who has lost a loved one becomes more compassionate and caring.

So on a particular day, I read all of Tom's poems. It was an excellent, heartfelt book. Tom was an extraordinary man with compassion in his heart.

Sadly, Tom died recently. He has now joined his loving wife. I regretted not comforting him and becoming the friend he desperately needed. When I see him again, I will hug him for a lifetime.

# CHAPTER 40

# HOW YOU SURVIVE

## YOU DO NOT RECOVER – YOU SURVIVE

I changed the subtitle of this book from "Recovering" to "Surviving and healing."

Through this journey, you realize that you may never fully recover from losing your child. The definition of recovery is getting back to where you were before. The final step to recovering is completely healing from an accident or a trauma. There is no full recovery when you lose your child. You will never be the person you were before, and you will carry that pain and hollowness inside you because, in your heart, you will always miss your child. So the better word is to survive, not to recover. You do survive but in a different mold. If you lose an arm or a leg, you endure and live without your arm or leg. There is no complete healing. The same is true about your heart. Part of your heart is gone and won't recover to its level before your child's death. It is impossible. Only people who have lost a child can fully understand that conclusion. So you move forward with a heavy heart, damaged beyond what you could have imagined. But you live on and pray for strength to find happiness and joy and strive to appreciate your life. You think about the family you still have supporting you and the children and grandchildren in the family who still love you. Everyone who understands Grief will understand what you are going through and will love you unconditionally.

## ANXIETY IS THE NEW NORMAL

My daughter always wanted to be calm and not be overwhelmed with her anxiety. She always worried about family members and friends and this would create fear within her through her worrying.

She loved with compassion and could not imagine life without her mom or me. She mentioned in a phone conversation that she would not know how to survive if she lost either of us. She feared our death and couldn't imagine life without us.

Ironically, our family endured the tragic loss of Amanda. So now we all live with new anxiety.

A bereaved parent will experience high anxiety during the first six months after a loved one's death. After that, there will be nights when you wake up in the middle of the night and tremble.

Sometimes my pillow was damp; sometimes, it was soaked. Sometimes it was dry, but more often than not, my bed was a disorganized mess. Your body is out of control, tossing and turning, weeping and shaking. It was my new normal during those earlier months. So now I understand the challenges my daughter experienced with her anxiety. You learn to meditate, to take those long and slow deep breaths to slow the heart and reduce stress.

## SLEEPING IS A NEW CONCEPT –
## EXHAUSTION PREVAILS

The anxiety that you might experience leads to sleepless nights. For me, it was a special worry. You know you have to eat well and sleep well. Sleeping reenergizes your body, but exhaustion was daily during the first six months. The sleeping was sporadic, even with sleeping aids. You realize it will take time to regain solitude through a good night's sleep.

So you accept it. It is Grief, and sleeping difficulties will be part of your journey. So you focus on remaining healthy by eating well and getting daily exercise, even if it is a walk in the park. You may be surprised you even have an appetite. I was physically sick and nauseous in the early days after learning of my daughter's death, not daily, but often. The shock and trauma were just too overbearing, making me physically ill.

As you sleep, you wish for that special dream. My first dream about Amanda was in my fifth month. You hope it is a positive dream with your loved one happy and safe. Unfortunately, my first dream wasn't positive. In this dream, Amanda was sad and alone. She spoke but without expression. A tear fell from her eyes. Her daughter Ellie was not in her life. The dream just ended. You pray for positive dreams or positive signs about your child. Sometimes these things fail to come to fruition.

Fortunately, a week later, a dream turned positive. The doorbell rang on a Sunday as my wife and I were getting ready for church. It was Amanda holding Ellie in her arms. She spoke! She said that she wanted to go to church with me. I said desperately, "Please talk to me some more!" You want to hear your child's voice one more time. She was silent and just looked at me. The dream ended shortly after that, but I saw her and heard her voice, even though it was just for a moment. You learn to accept the slightest positive signs when you grieve, which helps more than one can imagine.

## SEARCHING FOR HAPPINESS

When you experience acute grieving and prolonged mourning, the sadness is intense. You look at the intensity of Grief and don't see any light. There seems to be no escape from these feelings. But the intense feelings and emotions become easier to bear as time passes and you do the right things to heal.

My wife was supportive in many ways. She would cry and tell me she felt lost, sharing me with everyone else. She missed me. I was different, distant, and lived in a fog for many months. How could I tell my wife that I would never be happy again? How could I tell my other children that I would always be sad? When feelings are raw, this is your mindset. When you are in deep Grief, it is so powerful that it is scary. You become reluctant to tell the truth. You fear that people will think you have lost your healthy state of mind.

So what did I do? I will tell you this.

I had to embrace my Grief, accept it and understand that my emotions would emerge at unexpected times.

Once you embrace it and stop avoiding it, it will pass in time. You will begin to feel better. The second thing that helped me tremendously was to "count my blessings." We are all blessed in many ways. Even though our hearts are broken, there are many things to remember that bring joy.

You may have other children. Are they healthy? There are many things to consider, and once you start realizing all your other blessings, it may ease the pain of losing your child just a little bit.

Yes, tears will be your companion. You will drop many tears when you grieve hard, and these tears will be your salvation. It is healthy to grieve hard. It made me feel better after a good cry because I let God know how much this hurt.

So in searching for happiness, I trusted God's plan and believed I would see my child again someday. You think you're still on this earth for a reason, even though your child is gone. It was my only way to move forward and enjoy the remaining days of my life. We never know if tomorrow will come.

## REBUILDING AND REMEMBERING

When you feel it is time to rebuild, you must find something to help you survive this tragedy. It could be writing poems, doing artwork, building a collage, constructing a book of photographs, writing a journal, or doing anything that helps you keep calm and keep the memories of your child fresh in your mind. For me, it was writing and reading. Writing this book saved me from many dark thoughts. A bereaved parent often feels overwhelmed with emotion, and expressing your feelings on paper can be healthy. I remember lying in bed early at night with many thoughts and feelings. Those thoughts would continue throughout the sleep-less nights.

Waking up and starting to write became an obsession. I needed to get to my writing and put my thoughts and emotions on pa-per. The words just flew out of my head. I didn't have writer's block whatsoever. It was healthy for me to write. It was easier for me to write than to talk about it. It calmed me down and allowed me to open up the deep feelings of despair.

Anyone who loses a child will experience many emotions mentioned in this book. Hopefully, the experience I share with you will help you heal if you have lost a child. Unfortunately, men don't convey their feelings as well as women. As a result, men generally avoid conversations during these sensitive moments. However, not all men avoid these conversations. Some kindhearted men and women can be open and help you get through a rough day. A bereaved parent will explore avenues to remember their child. For me it was easier to dive deep into writing than to open up to male friends or acquaintances.

Remembering my precious daughter on this 27th day of the month. It has been eight months on this day, and we will forever miss her infectious smile and her love for her daughter, Ellie. We pray that she is at Peace. Our family will always remember and never forget the joy she brought to all of us.

## READING BOOKS ON GRIEF

By my ninth month, I had read many books on Grief and heaven and re-read several two or three times. It is hard to explain Grief's strength to someone who has not been through this kind of actual loss. You learn early that there is no particular way to grieve. Grief is unique to each person. It is dependent on so many things. The relationship you had with your child and how your child died. Was it unexpected, or was there a long illness? Did you have any chance to say goodbye? Was there suffering? Was it an act of violence? It doesn't matter the age of your child. It could be early in childhood, when your child was a baby, or it could be your child was a young adult. It could be that your child died in childbirth. It only matters that you lost your child. The Grief is enormous, no matter the age of your child or how your child died. For me, the loss resulted in mental and physical pain that is impossible to explain.

That is how we all feel with the loss of a child.

So the books helped me understand that I was not going crazy. You do not want to do the wrong things to survive, especially with acute Grief. I appreciated the advice and expertise these authors provided in their books. It was my escape in the evening. I could not wait to go into a room to read in the evening. I wanted to know more and wanted to feel better somehow. At times, the reading led to crying. When you read what you are going through, it hits home.

You say, "Yes, I have been going through all these emotions described in this book."

And then the tears flow. You feel weak and unable to function. You become disappointed in yourself. It was challenging to believe Grief could make a grown man cry so often, so hard, and for so long. But, after reading many stories about men and their Grief, you realize that being emotional, living, and experiencing pain is a strength, not a weakness. And no one can tell you differently. It takes accepting Grief's strength to let the tears flow and embrace the sadness.

## SUMMARY OF SOME THOUGHTS

These thoughts can be instrumental in moving past acute and complicated Grief. There is a need to find things that will get you through the difficult times. Finding comfort and understanding how to prepare for complex events is vital—following these can reduce anxiety so you can proceed with some joy.

### FINDING SOMETHING TO GET YOU THROUGH

- Find the right people to console you
- Explore new support – find new friends
- Pursue new avenues you haven't experienced before

### FINDING COMFORT – NOT IN THE PLACES YOU EXPECT

- Believe that signs from your loved one are real
- Even if you are not a writer, keep a journal and read to understand the Grief
- Manage your emotions with pictures and videos
- Give yourself time to rest
- Find a passion and a path to get to a safe place
- Open your eyes to stories of compassion and thankfulness

## DIFFICULT EVENTS AND ACTIVITIES

- Prepare early for difficult anniversaries, birthdays, and holidays.
- Protect yourself – figure out how to get through the most challenging situations
- Gain some energy to help each other – Children and Siblings – try hard
- Realize that enduring your loss  has no time limits – take the time you need
- Envision seeing some light at the end of the tunnel – you will see progress

# CHAPTER 41

# MOVING FORWARD

IT WILL BE a challenging journey, but with this Grief, you need to get through it. It's a long walk through a valley of despair. This statement may sound dramatic. But the pain is intense and brutal, and maybe it is surprising but oh, so true. My wife was more understanding and patient than ever before. The death of your child changes everything. It changed my motivation to zero, depleted my energy, and I feared it damaged some of my relationships by my extreme withdrawal and need to be alone, but I only imagined the damage. Everyone close to me understood the pain of what I had lost.

## GETTING TO THE OTHER SIDE OF GRIEF

How do you get to the other side of Grief?

Early on, you realize that Grief is a long journey, and you don't know if or when it will ever end. That is a debilitating thought; you feel so lost. So how do you get from mourning to joy? It starts with the process of surviving each day. You can't suppress Grief. You realize that you have to create a different life without your loved one who died. It's not a new life because a new life means that you leave it all behind you. You will never forget your child, but you realize that you can't continue living with the intense pain level. It gets physically and emotionally harmful.

My belief was not moving on but only moving forward. Moving forward is taking something with you. Moving on indicates leaving something behind. You realize that you will never leave the memory of your child behind. These are unbearable expectations. Everyone's journey is unique. It is unhealthy to avoid Grief and suppress the emotion. You accept the wailing and tears. The stages of Grief are not necessarily the same for everyone. There is no time limit, no formula that one must follow.

I remember praying for a time limit to my Grief. You want to know when the pain will end. Everyone grieves differently, and there should be no guilt about how you handle the sadness. It takes time to pick up the pieces and start living. No two relationships are the same. Your relationship with your loved one is unique. It gave me peace knowing that I would take all the time needed to survive and get well mentally and physically.

## YOUR BOND TO YOUR CHILD

People close to you mean well, but sometimes you might be offended. It is essential to understand that people mean well. I needed to tell people how close my relationship was with my child. Your attachment to your child and the nature of the relationship is unique. Your bond is exceptional, and the beauty of your relationship is a gift from God. I had faith; I believed that God knew about the joy of my relationship. God stays with you all the time. God always understands the relationship and the depth of your Grief. Having faith gave me peace of mind.

You cannot follow someone else's roadmap in dealing with Grief. It does not work, and it may not fit you. So I decided to visit the gravesite on a regular basis. Pictures and videos were my way of healing from Grief to remembering all the special moments. But you can't get overwhelmed looking at pictures and videos excessively, to the point of harm. You choose own your path. You can't compare your Grief to another person's Grief. Your time is your own; it becomes a precious thing to embrace.

## ACCEPTING THE REALITY OF LOSING YOUR CHILD

The most challenging hurdle was accepting the reality of losing my precious child. In my fifth month, my loss was apparent, but my heart could not accept this fact. As you read my daily journal, I kept repeating that I couldn't believe this had happened. Finally, you realize that your loved one is not coming back. It can be overwhelming. Your mind accepts it, but your heart doesn't. Your brain protects you in many ways. You have a distorted point of view. Your heart mourns for your beloved one and reaches a deep painful level never before experianced. Then the grieving follows.

Reality sets in after many months of Grief. It could last until the second year and the realization that your loved one is not returning.

> The numbness of the first year wears off, and in the second year, it comes back and expands. As a result, you may relive the trauma. You are blindsided with more Grief when a triggered memory causes extremely overwhelmed emotions.

It happens, and many different memories or events may blindside you. Most parents cannot prepare for this. For me, it was a simple smell, seeing someone who looked like my loved one, going to a store, memories of my child's favorite food, hearing that particular song, seeing something in the sky—it could be anything. It is the reality of Grief. So if you know what is coming your way, it may be easier to withstand.

## A QUESTION TO ASK YOURSELF

*Sit back and ask yourself, what would you give up to have your child back? Would you give up everything you own? Your home, your money, your success, your comfort of living? Would you live in poverty for the rest of your life? If you have a loving, strong, attached relationship with your child, most parents would give up everything for their child to return to earth and live their life again. Think about this and be honest with yourself. It will define your level of love for your child.*

## FOR YOU, MAYBE GOD IS THE ANSWER

I understand that many people may not believe or do not have faith. Preaching is not my intention. Everyone has thoughts on the afterlife and what the future holds for us. I embraced my weakened faith to gain traction by praying for God to give me the strength to endure the sadness. I visited holy places to calm down and reflect on what happened and why this happened to me, my daughter, and my family. Your world does change when your child dies before you ever expected it. It will change family dynamics. I prayed that grace would come to me. There are encouraging promises and amazing miracles in the Bible. Believing helped me understand that I was not alone in my Grief.

*Photo reference https://havenlight.com/collections/
yongsung-kim/products/the-hand-of-god-by-yongsung-kim*

In the Christian faith, one may need strength and God's help to gain a stronger belief. New friends may come into your life, and you may receive support from the most unexpected sources. As a result, it becomes critical to resist unhealthy forms of comfort, such as drugs and alcohol consumption.

It is essential to let others know the struggles of losing a child. In addition, it helps you heal by being honest with yourself and those closest to you.

## EXPRESSING YOUR EMOTIONS

Expressing your innermost emotions is a healthy way forward. As mentioned, you must believe this is a strength, not a weakness. Appropriately express your Grief and do it your way, whether in private or to a trusted friend or family member. You cannot numb your emotions or run away from deep feelings. You will find that you usually feel better after a good cry. If you suppress it, you may fail in the long run.

You will feel much different, and you will see yourself changing. So how do you see yourself? You are a bereaved parent now and are not the person you were before your child's death. As a result, people will see you in a different light. That can be a good thing, but you may come to realize that others may avoid you.

Grief scares many people, and it is difficult in our culture for some people to feel comfortable talking about or even acknowledging the death of their child. You will realize that you must carve out a new identity, but it may take time to redefine yourself.

## COMMITTING TO HEAL

When you commit to forging through this journey to get well, there are many turns and setbacks. Time will move more slowly than expected. It is agonizing to grieve. There may be others trying to rush you, and this is something you need to push back on for your wellbeing.

People don't want to see you stuck in your Grief. They want to make you happy again, and they all mean well. But you can't just get over it and move on from your life. You have to do those sentimental things that help you survive.

I kept some of my child's personal belongings and wanted to keep a few precious clothes. You may need to light candles, pray at church, or set aside private time to reflect on your love for your child.

Recommendations will come from friends and family who have good intentions. It would be best if you were gentle and appreciative of their suggestions.

You stay true to grieving at your timing and pace. People want to help you feel better. Sometimes you need solitude. Always make time for yourself, even if it means that others may not understand. A year or two down the road, you may still need to set aside time for yourself because you will never forget your child's love.

# CHAPTER 42

# THE DIFFICULT JOURNEY

IT IS A challenging, rugged, arduous journey. You become exhausted from being in pain after many months. The feeling of sadness and Grief for long periods is frustrating. You wish that it would just end and go away. A bereaved parent may question whether they are doing all the right things to get beyond the painful days. I often felt weak and was at a loss for what to do next. You think you can't even correctly grieve because it lasts so long. Being torn apart leaves you shattered, and it makes you feel lost.

When my daughter died, I didn't realize the grieving would be so intense for such a long time. Initially, you are out of control, traumatized, and in shock. Then that subsides but the loss and exhaustion set in for a long time.

Grief is hard work and takes a long time. How you handle it will either shorten or lengthen the timeline to get well emotionally.

Prepare for the intense early stages.

Sleep is most important. Sleep deprivation takes you down a difficult path.

I would play soothing music, try to eat well, and exercise to keep some muscle functionality. I went to the fitness center to get some cardio, move, walk, and jog. You must think about changes you must make, like your diet, and start to regain your mental balance through some light exercise. The mountain to climb is high and long.

## GET TO A DOCTOR

I was reluctant to get a checkup from my doctor. I finally went for my checkup; it was not good. The anxiety and Grief took their toll. The blood pressure rises, and the lack of sleep saps your energy and results in extreme fatigue. So I would recommend getting checkups from your doctor. Depending on your child's passing circumstances, there may be a difference in how long you grieve. My daughter died shockingly and unexpectedly, which extended my Grief. If your child was ill or endured a long sickness, maybe you prepared and grieved early. Advance grieving could result in a shorter Grief period because you have already suffered, but I don't know that firsthand. If your child was in an accident or died from a violent act, I imagine the Grief would be even more intense. Your world is now very different.

Sometimes you must avoid grieving to give yourself a break from the suffering to relieve the pain. For example, telling stories and talking about your loved one can be emotional, so I avoided doing this.

You are sad and want to look at pictures and videos, but sometimes you can't do it. You want to revisit where your child lived or spend time enjoying the outdoors, but you can't. Some day you will be able to go to places and see things that were difficult to visit early on. As additional time passes, visiting these places becomes more joyful, and you will smile. That is what we all desire, to be optimistic again and smile once in a while.

The wound takes time to heal, and sometimes it will reopen. I experienced new wounds that reopened, and the healing started over again. You have to be patient and take care of unexpected emotions. The level of exhaustion is difficult to put into words.

## YOUR CHILD'S BELONGINGS

Your child's belongings can bring such trauma to the heart when you have to go through the clothes and personal items that bring back memories. Collecting your deceased child's belongings can be very difficult, and you can delay all of this until the time is right. Timing is everything. Delaying can help you get through the Grief. You learn to go through these difficult moments at your own pace. You will realize you must progress and complete emotional tasks, but take small steps. I gathered some of my daughter's clothes, unique items, and the Bibles and journals she kept close to her. These items will always be with me. Amanda gave me a traveling coffee mug fifteen years ago. She was so excited to give it to me on my birthday. It cost her one dollar. I still have it today and use it frequently. It is a prized possession to keep forever in her memory.

## JOURNALING IS A GREAT OUTLET

As mentioned, I have read many books on Grief. Authors and health professionals strongly recommend starting a journal. It is an activity that provides benefits. It enables you to express your feelings and thoughts on paper. It is a release of emotions and memories that you may be unable to express outwardly.

Writing in a journal every day for many months resulted in this book. If you decide to write, go back to your early days of journaling to see the progress that you have made over time. Review what you have written. You will see and realize the difference between the early and later days. You will see progress. I was determined to publish this book in memory of my child. Writing was the best therapy for me. I would not have survived my days of Grief without writing about all my feelings. It was an enormous outlet for me.

# CHAPTER 43

# HOW LONG WILL THIS GRIEF LAST?

GRIEF WILL STAY with you longer than you desire, but the days get easier to survive as time passes. You will slowly feel better physically and mentally. There are many books regarding the length of Grief. "When will the Grief end? How long is too long?" Bereaved parents will always miss their lost loved ones. There are feelings of longing that will stay with you.. You desire not to forget your child. The critical point is not to let it consume you. It happens; you do not want those feelings to ever go away. You convince yourself to "be strong and more resilient." Being resilient when your heart is shattered is easier said than done. Your emotions result from your bond and relationship with your child.

You realize that you cannot go on with the intense pain. Some experts have said that the Grief from the death of a child may take five or more years to stabilize. When unexpected, a counselor mentioned that recovery could take years, not weeks or months. What is becoming stable? The first year was numbing, and everything was a blur. You endure all the holidays, birthdays, and family activities. It is an excruciating and overwhelming time. Nevertheless, your thoughts slowly turn toward the future.

After one year, more holidays, anniversaries, and birthdays will be challenging. The second Christmas can be more complicated than the first. Every grieving parent handles holidays differently. When you are in an acute grieving stage for a long time during that first year, you may not remember much about those first events and activities. Instead, you only remember being numb and going through the motions.

After reality sets in, you experience new emotions. However, you become more resilient because you slowly overcome the trauma of losing your child.

There will be better days. Of course, you never think that way initially, but the days become softer in your heart. You will always have your child in your heart even though you have begun life without them. You are on a journey, but the intensity of extreme Grief does not last forever.

There is another side to Grief and a healing process when dealing with family and friends. Of course, there will always be a sense of sadness, but as you heal, you will have emotional memories that will turn into historical memories. You will get through the journey as you survive your loss, but you will not forget the best memories with your child. Losing your child will partially break your heart, but you must move forward and believe you can live with happiness with your child on your shoulder. Your child will always be with you in spirit and memories.

## THE FINAL MONTHS OF THE FIRST YEAR

Just when you feel stronger and have made it through the most challenging moments during the first year, you can become overwhelmed with Grief at a moment's notice.

# "Continuing Bonds"

I read about the concept of "Continuing Bonds" on the Internet, which was helpful because when you grieve, it is difficult to let go of your child, and a bereaved parent has extreme difficulty accepting death. You always desire to keep that bond with your child.

*Reference; https://whatsyourGrief.com/continuing-bonds-shifting-the-Grief-paradigm/*

Grief is described in this way: When your loved one dies, it isn't about working through a linear process that ends in "acceptance" or a new life, where you have moved on or have compartmentalized your loved one's memory.

Instead, when a loved one dies, you slowly find ways to adjust and redefine your relationship with that person, allowing for a continued bond that will endure, in different ways and to varying degrees, throughout your life. This relationship is not unhealthy, nor does it mean you are not grieving in a usual way.

Instead, the continuing bonds theory suggests that this is normal and healthy and that an essential part of Grief is continuing ties to your loved one in this way. Rather than assuming detachment as a normal Grief response, continuing bonds consider natural human attachment, even in death.

# CHAPTER 44
# THOUGHTS OF MORTALITY

A BEREAVED PARENT begins to think about their mortality. We have heard the common phrase that "tomorrow is not promised to anybody." However, once you have experienced the loss of your child, you recognize and fully understand there may be no tomorrow. Do you care? Early on in Grief, you do not care.

During the first couple of months of losing a child, you do not care about dying; there were times I wanted to relieve the mental pain by not waking up in the morning. The pain of your child passing and never being able to see your child again is more intense than a human being can imagine. You only want to see your child in heaven again. You don't think of all the consequences for your family or other children.

It's a surreal thought that doesn't make sense but it happens. Not caring is Grief at its worst.

## IMPORTANCE OF TAKING CARE OF YOUR HEALTH

There is a reason you have to take care of your mental and physical health.

The loss of a child has lasting effects on the parents' health. Doing everything you can to reduce stress over time, engaging in counseling, exercising, and maintaining a good diet are all essential. The distress over the loss of a child carries sadness for the rest of our lives.

The key to recovery is to embrace the sorrow and focus on the positive, happy memories you shared with your child. I want to share a study addressing the mortality of bereaved and non-bereaved parents.

## "MORTALITY IN BEREAVED PARENTS"

*Reference: Mortality in parents after the death of a child – Science Direct. https://www.sciencedirect.com/science/article/pii/S0277953619305167*

The death of a child is one of the most traumatic life events, taking a considerable toll on the mental and physical health of parents (e.g., Stroebe, Schut, & Stroebe, 2007). National data from Sweden showed that a vast majority of older bereaved parents (85%) retrospectively reported the death of a child as the most critical negative life stressor they had ever experienced (Bratt, Stenstrom, & Renmark, 2018).

Other international studies have consistently found more significant mortality in bereaved parents relative to non-bereaved parents (Cohen-Mansfield et al., 2013; Harper et al., 2011; Li et al., 2003; Rostila, Saarela, & Kawachi, 2012; Schorr et al., 2016), regardless of socioeconomic status, age, and race (Cohen-Mansfield et al., 2013; Schorr et al., 2016).

The data on the cause of parent death show relatively high death rates due to heart disease, which implicates chronic stress as a possible mechanism for parent mortality. In addition, prior research has found that chronic stresses in adulthood impact the development or progression of cardiovascular disease in individuals via acute stress response and pathophysiological changes over time.

Accordingly, the high death rates due to heart disease in the current sample of bereaved parents suggest that the chronic stress associated with parental bereavement across midlife and early old age might be an essential contributor to early mortality in bereaved parents.

## Cause of death in bereaved parents

Researchers have also examined the cause of death in parents. Schorr et al. (2016) found that in the decades after the death of a child, coronary heart disease was a significant cause of death for bereaved mothers and circulatory disease was a major cause of death for bereaved mothers and bereaved fathers.

## Study Results

The present study suggests that the death of a child has lasting adverse impacts on the risk of early mortality in bereaved parents, net of their sociodemographic characteristics and genetic predisposition. As Rogers et al. (2008) noted, the effects of Grief after the death of a child might be challenging to detect in daily role functioning (e.g., work, socializing), but they nevertheless take a toll in the form of long-term health consequences.

# CHAPTER 45

# ENDURING GRIEF

THIS CHAPTER CLARIFIES those mired in prolonged Grief. Getting past and accepting a child's death can become an agonizing ordeal. Even after an entire year, the yearning can remain intense. Bereaved parents wonder why they cannot control these emotions. The mentally strong mother or father becomes weakened by the strength of Grief. Despite being less intense and less frequent, setbacks might continue.

## RESILIENT GRIEF OR COMPLICATED GRIEF

Fortunately, the intensity and frequency lessen, but they remain. Mary-Frances O'Conner, Ph.D., in her book *The Grieving Brain: The surprising science of how we learn from Love and Loss*, stated the physiological effects of Grief through her detailed years of study with participants who had a significant loss in their lives.

In layman's terms, some parents are more resilient in their Grief when they lose a child than others who enter into a path of "Complicated Grief." Those who do not get stuck in Grief or do not have prolonged periods of emotional distress realize early on that the loss is final and is the order of things in life. As a result, they are resilient and handle death in a less complicated emotional way.

Everyone is different, and we all take significant losses uniquely personally. There is no right or wrong way to grieve.

Those who experience complicated Grief in response to remind-ers of the deceased loved one do so because they continue to yearn to see them again, as we do for living loved ones. They be-lieve that losing a child is not the correct order of things. There is an apparent yearning to see or hear about their loved one.

Biological and chemical reasons exist for those who experience "Complicated Grief." O'Conner's study distinguished one dif-fering brain region between the complicated Grief and resilient group. The region is called the "Nucleus Acumens." The Nucleus Acumens (NAc) is a significant component of the brain and is a fundamental structure in mediating emotional processes.

The group with complicated Grief showed greater activation in this brain region than the more resilient group.

The brain releases certain hormones during specific bouts of trauma and shock. In addition, there are receptors and neu-rons in the brain that are released when triggered during Grief. Studies have shown that there may be a link to genetic variations in the brain's receptors that put people at risk for developing complicated Grief.

This study helped me understand how the brain controls many emotions that seem difficult to manage through acute Grief.

Yearning episodes and emotional setbacks are more intense if your relationship with your child is loving and strong—i.e., the closer your relationship with your child, the greater your feelings of despair. The reason a bereaved parent feels out of control is sometimes an endless search for relief.

It is common for bereaved parents to feel out of control and yearn to see their lost child. However, realizing they cannot see their child again in the future results in extreme longing and emptiness.

## WHY DOES GRIEF CONTROL YOUR EMOTIONS?

The deep encoding of our loved ones in our brains is powerful. It has a powerful effect on our behavior, motivation, and feelings. These powerful tools include hormones, neural connections, and genetics, which may even override the obvious painful knowledge that the loved one is no longer alive. (*The Grieving Brain*, O'Conner, Chapter 6, page 122)

## HOW A CHRISTIAN PARENT HANDLES THE DEATH OF A CHILD

*This exceptional excerpt is copyrighted and describes the Christian views related to a bereaved parent.*

© Copyright 2002-2022 Got Questions Ministries. All rights reserved.  *Permission to use approved as referenced.*

As parents, we cannot imagine a more traumatic experience than the death of a child. All parents naturally expect their children to outlive them. Such a loss is an extraordinary, out-of-order event that brings overwhelming pain and lingering Grief. It is a life-altering experience that presents unique challenges to parents as they seek to rebuild their lives without their children.

It would be presumptuous for anyone to tell parents how to handle the death of a child. However, those who yield their lives to God are more apt to recover from such a loss. There is a greater sense of normalcy than those without genuine and optimistic faith. So, with this being true, how do Christian parents handle the death of a child? Does the Bible address the subject, and if so, in what way?

First, we should note that each person handles Grief differently. Emotions vary widely in their intensity. These emotions are normal and natural. Second, no parent ever "gets over" or "moves on" from the death of a child. It is not like an illness from which we recover.

Most counselors liken it to a life-changing physical injury. However, we should also know that, though we may always feel the loss, its intensity does diminish with time.

The Christian faith in a loving and ever-faithful God enables us to endure and recover from the death of a child, sometimes in ways that others find remarkable. Such was the case of David in the loss of his child, who died seven days after birth **(2 Samuel 12:18–19)**. Several valuable lessons from this passage of Scripture help grieving parents understand and face the future with hope.

One is that David prayed fervently for his child's life **(2 Samuel 12:16)**. This should be true for all parents and not just when times are difficult. Parents should always pray for their children, asking God to watch them and protect them. Likewise, parents should pray that God provides godly wisdom and guidance so that their children grow in the nurture and admonition of the Lord (*Judges 13:12; Proverbs 22:6; Ephesians 6:4*).

Another lesson we learn from David is his reaction to his child's death. Upon learning that the infant had died, there was an acceptance signified by his actions when he "arose from the ground, washed and anointed himself, and changed his clothes; and he went into the house of the LORD and worshiped. Then he went to his own house; and when he requested, they set food before him, and he ate" (*2 Samuel 12:20*). What is surprising about this passage is that David "went into the house of the Lord and worshiped." In other words, David not only accepted the death of his child, but he gave it all over to God in worship. The ability to worship and honor God in a time of trial or crisis is a powerful demonstration of our spiritual confidence in God. Doing so enables us to accept the reality of our loss.

Furthermore, this is how God frees us to go on living; what David models for us in this story is learning to turn loose what we cannot change.

The next lesson is the most revealing. It is confidence in the knowledge that children who die before they reach the age of accountability go to heaven. David's response to those questioning his reaction to the death of his child has always been a great source of comfort to believing parents who have lost infants and young children. "But now that he is dead, why should I fast? Can I bring him back again? I will go to him, but he will not return to me" (*2 Samuel 12:23*). David was confident that he would meet his son in heaven. This passage indicates that babies and young children who pass from this world will go to heaven.

Grieving the death of a child is a heartrending journey. Unfortunately, there are no hard and fast rules or guidelines to teach us how to handle our mourning.

However, counselors and those who have experienced the loss of a child have provided some helpful advice.

"Do not put time limits on your recovery. Do not expect a day to pass without thinking about your child, nor should you want to."

# CHAPTER 46

# THE FINAL DAY OF THE FIRST YEAR

IT WAS THE day before the first anniversary of my daughter's death—a day to remember, for sure. As I drove to the cemetery that day, to my surprise, the truck carrying my daughter's headstone was turning into the cemetery right in front of me. Seeing the name "Ross" on the gravestone in the back of the truck made me numb. It was six months since we ordered the headstone, and now, the day before the first anniversary, it was to be installed. I did not wish to sit there and watch them install my daughter's gravestone. I drove away and returned a few hours later to tidy up the site. I decided to return to the cemetery alone. These challenging days are complicated, and you never know how you will react. Your mind and body are not in a steady state. I pulled up a chair beside Amanda's grave, alone, with no one else present at the cemetery.

It had been a while since the tears flowed, but it was another meltdown. It was OK. It was my time to grieve until there was complete exhaustion. I spent the next few hours resting my soul and staying calm. Finally, you feel relieved because you now know tears have a healing effect on the human body. So this was my last day of the first year. Once again, bereaved parents pray for strength, resilience, and staying positive, moving to a future without their loved ones.

## My Final Social Media Post One Year Anniversary

One year today, our family lost you, Amanda. But we will continue to gain the strength to survive each day. The year has gone by fast, yet at times, the days have been slow as family tears continue to flow. God bless you, Amanda. We now hold your memory close to us every day. Ellie is our salvation, and we will take care of her and keep you in Ellie's memory forever.

## Final Reflections

Reflecting on the first year after my daughter died, I realize there is a healthy way forward, even if you never believe that you will be happy again. You are traumatized and feel crippled beyond repair when you lose a child. Thinking about my Grief, it would have been beneficial if I had pursued professional help to overcome the initial trauma and shock. The trembling lasted every day for 90 days. The physical shaking was out of control.

However, doctor-prescribed medicine proved to be effective in reducing extreme anxiety.

Based on several studies, doctors and Grief counselors believe that the death of a child always involves traumatic Grief. Therefore they highlight the importance of counselors assessing trauma symptoms that are present after the loss. Some suggest addressing trauma work before working on Grief and loss issues. I survived the physical and emotional trauma with the support of my wife, family, and friends, but it lasted a significant amount of time.

You get into modes of searching for meaning and purpose in life. You wonder what kind of person you will become. Questioning my purpose was a central focus of my journey early on. My child's tragic and untimely loss made it difficult to fit the death experience into future thoughts. How could I be happy again without my child? Trying to be happy again became an overwhelming search for my new purpose in life.

Finding purpose led to an intense search to understand the loss and more significant existential issues such as the purpose of life and death.

As a bereaved parent, you wonder how you can live after losing your loved one. I became highly focused on "life after death" and believed there was an afterlife. Believing in the afterlife helped me to survive my worst days. It is all spelled out in the Bible.

Did I experience long-term "Complicated Grief?" It seemed so.

It was difficult for me to ACCEPT the loss of my daughter well into the end of the first year. Unfortunately, I was constantly emotional early on, mostly in private and several times in public. However, I healed by embracing the sorrow, not suppressing the excessive emotions, and realizing Grief did not have a necessary end date. It wasn't easy to function normally. However, I felt better after a good cry.

*A definition of Complicated Grief defined in Webster's dictionary.*

Complicated Grief is a state of mourning in which Grief reactions are intense, enduring, and interfere with your ability to function in daily life. It involves lasting separation distress, meaninglessness, difficulty accepting the loss, and difficulties moving on in life.

You focus on surviving and managing the many emotions during the most challenging days. Accepting the death of a loved child takes a longer time than expected. You turn to your faith, feeling that you will ultimately be reunited with your child and realizing that life is short and death is inevitable.

# CHAPTER 47

---

# CONCLUDING THOUGHTS

THERE IS *"NO GREATER PAIN."* Grief takes many forms, so be prepared for a long journey. Many authors write books about Grief but have not experienced the most tremendous loss of all—the unexpected loss of a child. It changes a bereaved parent's world, and it takes substantial time to accept a significant loss. It takes time to envision life without a loved one. Looking into the future, many years without their child's presence is mind-boggling.

The mind and heart do not accept it.

It takes more time than can be imagined.

It is a heartbreaking adjustment to the way we think. However, we eventually realize this fact, which is not easy to accept. Therefore, it would be best to acknowledge it in order to move forward one step at a time.

The harder you love, the harder you grieve. In the end, love conquers everything. It is all about love. It is essential to survive and, most importantly, love God.

This is the honest truth. The duration of Grief will depend on the closeness of the relationship. Those who love hard will grieve hard, and nothing else matters. A bereaved parent does not care what people think about it being time to "move on." Nevertheless, they can never move on the same as they were before. A bereaved parent is now changed forever. They will do whatever is necessary to survive and be happy again.

## THE SHOCK OF REREADING MY BOOK

When I began writing my thoughts daily, the weeks and months passed, and my journal lengthened. Early on, you are in a fog most of the time, expressing your feelings about losing your precious child. After finishing my writing, I reread my journal from the beginning to the end, and it shocked me. When you experience shock and trauma, your memory goes haywire. You don't remember how you acted. You don't see how you changed or realize how weak you were in the face of Grief. I was somewhat embarrassed about my vulnerability in handling my daughter's loss. It was such an emotional year, day after excruciating day. I wasn't resilient or strong like most men would seem to be in the face of shock and despair.

My mourning and grieving developed into "complicated Grief" described in many books. When you have deep-rooted love for your child, the weight of Grief brings the most resilient fathers and strong-willed mothers to their knees when they realize they will never see their child again. It is the weight no human can endure when you have a close relationship with and deep love for your child. You think you will not make it through, but you manage the Grief and come out of this ordeal a different person. You feel different and look at the days ahead in another way. You learn to appreciate what you have and may always have the longing and yearning for your child. It becomes more manageable as the months and years pass by.

**This is the unspoken truth about Grief.**

## FEELING THE RAIN

I will share another example of how grieving can encourage you to appreciate the simple things in life that may bring you some peace and relaxation.

When you grieve, you do things you may have never done before. For example, have you ever walked in the rain? Have you ever walked outside and let the warm rain fall on you until you are soaking wet?

When it rains on a warm summer evening, think about the beauty of the water falling from the sky. Walk outside in the rain, and let yourself become drenched by the water falling out of the clouds. While experiencing exhausting Grief, I walked outside into the rain, looked up into the sky, and prayed for strength to ease the pain. Just let the rain soak your face and open your eyes to see the raindrops fall to the ground. It is a cleansing, refreshing experience. It is nature at its best. We live in a world so unpredictable that when you get sidetracked in life, and the order of things makes no sense, you pray for strength. When you lose a child, you give your soul to God because you must surrender to the weight of Grief. The morning sunshine is enlightening, but there is something about the rain that soothes your soul.

## EXPERIENCING NATURE AND THE WORLD AROUND US

For so many years, my eyes were not fully open to the natural surroundings on this earth. Now, through pain, trauma, and Grief, I have opened my eyes to see and appreciate the magnificent landscapes, mountains, and abundance of cloud formations in my state of Maryland that have become a breathless sight to behold. Looking up at the sky in the evenings, you can see sunsets that are unimaginable works of art. The clouds have openings that let the beams of light shine through, making them look like the gates of Heaven. Tree formations capture the picture of a heart. Glistening sunshine on lakes in the mountains brings serenity to one's heart. The dramatic weather changes make you realize we are not in control. However, the weather, landscapes, and skies are all created for us to enjoy. Looking at where we live and appreciating the nature around us is the best medicine for the soul.

## REALIZING THERE IS A NEW NORMAL

With all the emotions one experiences, a new normal for a bereaved parent is moving forward with compassion. So naturally, a bereaved parent will feel and act differently as a result of the heartbreaking loss of a child. Of course, not all parents feel all of these emotions, but many do. These resonate with me in my experience with complicated Grief, and there is truth to it all. It is a cross we all bear, and we have the resilience to enjoy life but carry our loved ones in our hearts at a level that is difficult to explain. So please understand that when you meet a bereaved parent, they are compassionate and strong. Do not feel sorry for us, as we live in a different standard and move forward, enjoying and appreciating all we have.

## A BED FOR MY HEART

This excerpt was written and published by *A Grieving Mother It takes a village. Reference ABedForMyHeart.com*

# — WHAT IS NORMAL AFTER YOUR CHILD DIES? —

- Normal is having tears waiting behind every smile because your child is missing from all the important events in your life.

- Normal is feeling like you can't sit for another minute without getting up because you don't like to sit through anything anymore.

- Normal is not sleeping very well because a thousand what if's & why didn't I's go through your head constantly.

- Normal is reliving the day your child died continuously through your eyes and mind, holding your head to make it go away.

- Normal is each year coming up with the difficult task of how to honor your child's memory and their birthdays and survive these days.

- Normal is a heartwarming and yet sinking feeling at the sight of something special your child loved.

- Normal is having some people afraid to mention your child.

- Normal is weeks, months, and years after the initial shock, the grieving may get worse, not better.

- Normal is not listening to people compare anything in their life to your loss, unless they have lost a child. Nothing compares.

☙ Normal is realizing you do cry not every day but many days.

☙ Normal is asking God why he took your child's life instead of yours.

☙ Normal is learning to lie to everyone you meet and telling them you are fine. You lie because it makes others uncomfortable if you cry. You've learned it's easier to lie to them than to tell them the truth that you still feel empty and lost.

☙ And last of all...

☙ Normal is hiding all the things that have become "normal" for you to feel - but you move forward with new resolve and strength to live life to its fullest.

# CHAPTER 48

# 14 THINGS I LEARNED SINCE LOSING MY CHILD

IN MY TESTIMONIAL, I mentioned that child loss is like no other. Unfortunately, it is a loss that is often misunderstood by many. Here is what I've learned within one year of Grief, trekking through the unimaginable. I believe that most bereaved mothers and fathers will experience some of these same feelings.

Angela Miller has published some of these statements. Along with excerpts from her work, I included three of the ones I have experienced.

Reference https://abedformyheart.com/7-things-since-loss-of-child/

## 1. REMEMBERING THE INITIAL SHOCK

You will never forget the finite details of the day you learned of your child's death. The sequence of events is etched permanently in your mind. You will remember where you were, the time of day, and the trauma that followed. There is no way around it. Years may pass by, and you will still remember that horrible day. You will remember the trembling, the loss of control, and the long-term sadness. It has become a part of your history and part of your soul.

## 2. ONLY 5 MINUTES

As you remember that day, you may also experience the strongest desire to have five more minutes with your child. You will have this longing and heartbreaking wish to see your child again to tell them how much you love them and how proud you are as a caring and compassionate mother or father. The ache in your heart stays with you with these thoughts. You think of everything you want to express, enjoy one more hug, and hear your child's voice.

My daughter would tell me how deep her love was for our whole family; if something ever happened to us, she could not live a happy life. How ironic that seems to be. Here I sit today, alive and well, while my daughter lies in her coffin in her grave in the cemetery just one mile away from me. Not being able to see, touch, or hear your deceased child is agonizing. A bereaved parent would give up anything to have that five minutes with their child just one more time.

## 3. LEARNING THE TOTAL VALUE OF APPRECIATING BLESSINGS

My priorities changed. Many things that were important to me no longer are. Material things do not matter. You begin to feel more sorrow than ever for less fortunate people. You want to help in many ways. You begin to see beauty in things you never noticed before, "take it all in," and appreciate the simplest things in life. My daughter died with very little money to her name. She spent it all on her daughter and enjoyed the simple things in life. She was content to be with her daughter. The "dollar store" was her favorite place, and it was surprising how excited it made her feel when she bought simple things.

Now I understood how she felt. When you lose your child, your world changes; counting my blessings helped me move forward when it seemed impossible to survive the day. If you focus on all the blessings in your life, you realize that you are fortunate in many ways. When you pick up the pieces from losing your child, you can get past the uncontrollable emotions and feel alive again with your child's shadow on your shoulders.

## 4. LOSS OF THE FEAR OF DEATH

When your child dies, the thoughts of your own death take center stage. When my child died, my fear of death all but disappeared. Instead, I experienced feelings of excitement to see my daughter again in the afterlife. You later realize that it is the trauma of the brain that sidetracks you from everyday thoughts. Your mind draws you into this strange way of thinking. Not many things can bring a person to a place where they have no fear of death, but losing a child can result in having no fear. Unfortunately, the pain runs so deep that you do not envision the destruction you would leave behind with other family members, other children, your spouse, and grandchildren if you died. You believe God has His plan for all of us.

You become determined to live your life searching for joy because your loved one would want you to move on even though the sadness is understood. The new normal is moving forward with a healthy and profound sadness. One can carry both sorrow and joy together. Finding joy in any form is the only way to survive going forward.

## 5. GREATER COMPASSION FOR OTHERS

You learn more about unspeakable compassion and giving when presented with deep sorrow. Though you will grieve your loved one's death forever and then some, it does not mean your life will lack happiness and joy. Quite the contrary—after I survived acute Grief, and it took me a long time to get there, I now live from a deeper place. As a result, my attempts to care are more profound and effortless. Grief enhances your senses and awareness of many things. You learn to cherish those times when there are small amounts of joy.

You claw your way from the depths of unimaginable pain, suffering, and sorrow, again and again– when the joy comes, however– it is a joy to embrace. When a gift or an act of kindness came my way, I became emotional and thankful because there is nothing– and I mean absolutely nothing– I take for granted now. Living life in this way will give you peace.

## 6. LOVE NEVER DIES

There will never come a day, hour, minute, or second that you stop loving or thinking about your loved one. Just as parents of living children unconditionally love their children always and forever, so do bereaved parents. I love my child just as much as you love yours–the only difference is that mine lives in heaven. Unfortunately, our culture becomes uncomfortable about discussing children gone too soon. It was not easy to talk about my daughter initially because it was challenging to get through the emotions. However, as you pray for more strength, there comes a time when it will not stop you from saying your daughter's name and sharing her love and light everywhere you go.

My daughter's life was cut irreversibly short, but her love lives on forever. The one thing that overcomes everything is the love for your child. It is more potent than anyone who has not lost a child could imagine. The unimaginable becomes a reality, with it you gain strength and compassion for a lifetime.

## 7. YOU WILL GRIEVE FOR A LIFETIME

Period. The end.

There is no "moving on" or "getting over it." You have to manage it and work through the pain. There is no bow, fix, or solution to this heartache. There is no end to how you will grieve and how long you will grieve. There is no glue for your broken heart, no medicine for the pain, and no going back in time. You will suffer and ache as you breathe and love your child with all your heart and soul.

The bereaved parent wishes that people could understand that Grief lasts forever because love endures forever; the loss of a child is not one finite event; it is a continuous loss that unfolds minute by minute throughout a lifetime.

A bereaved parent will miss every birthday, holiday, milestone, and life's success to be shared. Some weddings will never be; a mother and father's pride and excitement seeing their child grow and flourish are gone – an entire generation of people are irrevocably altered. Missing the future is why Grief lasts forever. The ripple effect lasts forever. The bleeding only slows but never stops. You move forward with an injured heart.

## 8. EMPTINESS IS ALWAYS PRESENT

During the moments of celebration, birthdays, and family events, joy will come back into your life, and you will begin to live again. However, that empty chair, an empty room, or a space never becomes less empty. There is an emptiness in every family picture, but you grasp onto the good memories.

Empty spaces are now constant reminders. There will always be a missing space in your life and a forever hole in your heart. Time does not heal or make the space less empty. Neither do encouragements or wishes for us to "move on" from well-intentioned family or friends.

You try to look at it a different way, but empty is still empty. Missing is still missing. Gone is still gone. The problem is that there is nothing that can fix it. Minute after heartbreaking minute, hour after hour, day after day, month after month, and year after year, the space remains. The length of our missing child lasts a lifetime. Thus, we rightfully miss them forever. It is crucial for everyone who has not lost a child to understand this.

## 9. SPECIAL EVENTS AND HOLIDAYS MAY ALWAYS BE COMPLEX

No matter how long it has been, holidays may never become easier without your loved one. Nevertheless, you strive to find peace and embrace the love of a family because everyone understands the loss. However, unfortunately, some people may never understand and may feel frustrated at your continued struggle with grieving. Have you ever wondered why every holiday season is torture for a bereaved parent, even if it has been

1, 2, 5, or 10 years later? It is because they really, genuinely are still grieving. Imagine having to live every holiday without one or more of your precious children. Imagine how that might feel for you. Losing an arm or a leg is more manageable than living without your flesh and blood. Almost anything would be easier than living without one or more of your precious children.

That is why holidays are always and forever hard for bereaved parents. Do not wonder why or even try to understand. Know that you do not have to understand to be a supportive presence.

When family and friends support and love you as a bereaved parent during the holiday season, it will be the best gift you could ever receive.

## 10. CLOSER RELATIONSHIP WITH LIVING CHILDREN AND SPOUSE

As you search for salvation and blessings, you may have other children and family members you have ignored, set aside, or just kept your distance from while you felt disillusioned or so distraught that nothing else mattered. Loneliness is what acute Grief has done to you. However, unfortunately, you may have caused collateral damage during your Grief to the people most important to you.

Now you have the strength to make amends. You learn to keep moving forward, even with setbacks. So now, after a long time, you are ready to focus on your other children, your grandchildren, your significant other, your spouse, or other family members. Through all the pain, you have learned to appreciate those you have in your life, and you grow even closer than before.

These setbacks are expected and normal, but they make you stronger. So it is not the end when your child dies; you believe it is another beginning in your life, and you carry your child's love with you every step.

## 11. THE LIGHT BRIGHTENS; YOU SURVIVE AND FLOURISH

There is intense Grief throughout the first six months before the numbness begins to subside. You think that you can never be happy again. Unfortunately, not visualizing happiness seems to be initially true for all grieving parents.

You become a new person. You realize that you can survive anything. Big things that used to cause significant stress now become small things. Small things that used to irritate you become nonexistent. Everything has changed. You carry your love for your child everywhere. You feel bonded and realize that your child wants you to live joyfully even though your child is no longer with you.

The aching pain in your chest, high anxiety, and uncontrollable emotions subside, and you feel that you have made it. You made it through hell, and now you start living each day like it may be your last—no more judging, anger, or worries about what people may think of you. You now move forward with more resolve, strength, and compassion than you could have imagined. You have been to hell, and now you are back. God holds us tight and provides love and support when we need it most.

The devil has lost, and you are proud to skirt the evil temptations presented to you during acute Grief. Yes, if you are a bereaved parent, you can make it when you never thought you could. We are all unique now, and you move forward with pride and compassion for others.

## 12. GRIEF REALLY IS ALL-CONSUMING

There are strong emotions you may experience that may surprise you. As you accept your loss, these intense reactions result from setbacks you may encounter and fear that you are out of control.

A bereaved parent is not proud of the uncontrolled emotions during many months of grieving. I was embarrassed during multiple public meltdowns. However, the shock and sadness last a long time and enhance those more expressive emotions.

There is a build-up of anger and resentment from the tragedy of losing your child. The anger within you can be scary. Your body swells, your mouth becomes dry, your heart feels like it is going to burst, your body shakes uncontrollably, and your voice disappears from the anguish you express verbally. It is a scary time, and this is why bereaved parents feel out of control. The finality of losing your child is disheartening; it becomes that permanent scar you must carry for the rest of your life.

You learn how to calm down. You learn to think about those positive thoughts. You learn to take a step back and take a deep breath when you feel out of control, especially in anger. Your only salvation is to carry on and believe that your child is safe and living in a better place, without pain.

## 13. REALIZING THE WEIGHT OF GRIEF

This story summarizes the weight of Grief. Of course, you can't hold onto it forever. But there will be a time when you realize that you can't continue to let the weight of Grief destroy you.

*Written by Lee Ann Livingston, Spiritual care provider - Reference; Hospicecommunitycare.org/weight of grief/ website:*

Once upon a time, a wise teacher walked around the classroom teaching stress management. As she walked and talked, she carried in her hand a glass of water. When she stopped and raised the glass of water, the students were sure they would be asked if it was half full or half empty. So imagine the students' surprise when the wise teacher, with a smile on her face, asked, "How heavy is this glass of water?"

The wise teacher received various answers to her query, ranging from 8 ounces to 20 ounces. Finally, the wise teacher responded, "The absolute weight doesn't matter. It depends on how long you hold it. If you hold it for a minute, it's not a problem. If you hold it for an hour, you'll have an ache in your arm. If you hold it for a day, your arm will feel numb and paralyzed. In each case, the weight of the glass doesn't change, but the longer you hold it, the heavier it becomes."

As she continued, the wise teacher concluded her remarks by reminding her audience that the glass of water is like the stress or worries in life. Think about them for a while, and nothing much happens. Think about them a bit longer, and they begin to hurt. And if you think about them all day long, you'll feel paralyzed – incapable of doing anything. It becomes impossible if you hold that glass for weeks, months, or years.

Quite an interesting story, isn't it? The wise teacher had good words to help deal with life's stresses and worries. There is an appropriate connection with Grief in the wise teacher's words. If we see the glass of water as one of the many components of Grief, we may see the impact Grief can have upon us.

Grief is a normal response to our losses in life. The greater our loss, the greater our Grief weighs on our lives. In the death of a loved one, our memories become significant components of our Grief. Grief is most potent with a loss of a child. We replay our memories repeatedly; they are easily ignited when you recall past moments.

Memories are not only expected in Grief; they are necessary. It's the way we use our Grief memories that makes a difference. Like the glass of water, the longer we hold on to a memory, the heavier it can become. The power we give our memories makes the difference in our ability to favorably celebrate and enjoy our memories or allow them to weigh us down.

Good Grief involves putting our memories to work for us as we move through our Grief. Our memories can empower us to discover who we are in our loss and how we will live after our loss. Unfortunately, our memories can hinder our movement through Grief. It is up to us to give memory its proper perspective. Carrying regret does not help move through Grief. Such a memory may need to be acknowledged and let go in remembering; however, it often returns, giving a measure of forgiveness when needed.

The memories that show respect, dignity, joy, and insight into your new relationship with your lost loved one will be the memories you will want to keep close by, for they will give you strength. As with the glass of water in the wise teacher's hand, the weight of the memory never changes, but the length of time we choose to hold the memory makes all the difference.

One crucial final point: This "once upon a time" story doesn't end with "and they lived happily ever after." That ending may or may not be the case, for it depends on each individual and how they choose to navigate their Grief.

## 14. SIGNS FROM YOUR LOVED ONE

When you learn of your child's death, there is an instantaneous search for hope and belief that you will see your child again. You hope for signs that are unique to you and your child. A bereaved parent first sees signs as a coincidence, then as they repeat themselves, the coincidence becomes something to believe. A non-bereaved parent may think these signs are just one's imagination. However, when your heart breaks, you genuinely believe in God and the afterlife; you do believe in signs from your child. There are many instances of seeing and hearing signs unique to your child. My wife, my son, my daughter, and my former wife have all seen signs that are so unique to Amanda's being. One believes these signs are real and guide them toward peace and serenity, moving forward without their loved one. Most bereaved parents see these signs and live their daily lives with their hearts on their sleeves.

Some examples of signs from Heaven that a deceased loved one is with you; butterflies flying around you, visits from birds, seeing a dragonfly, finding items in strange places, sensing their presence, lights flickering or images appearing randomly, hearing music or their favorite song, and most notable is having dreams of your loved one.

# CHAPTER 49

# A LETTER SPOKEN FROM HEAVEN

AN AUTHOR WROTE a heartfelt message for those who have suffered a significant loss as they move forward on this challenging path without their loved one: "A letter from Heaven." This message reflects thoughts from your child and is a testament to hope. Your thoughts will guide you as you try to meet the challenge of living without your child. I hope this will give you peace that your child is safe and sees you moving forward. So embrace these thoughts and know you can survive as your child would want you to live your life.

## LETTER FROM HEAVEN...

Reference: https://emkarblog.com/2017/08/21/letter-from-heaven/

**Dear Mom and Dad,**

Now that I am in Heaven, I know that life for you isn't the same. I want you to know that I hear you say every day how much you miss me and love me. Yes, I still listen to you. I love you so much too. My love for you will never waver from Heaven. I know it is hard to continue when you feel you are walking through life without me, but I want you to know that I am right next to you. I walk through your life with you, guiding and helping you along the way. Our relationship never ended when I graduated to Heaven; it is simply different now. Heaven is all around you. Heaven is genuinely only three feet off your floor.

Please look for the signs that I leave for you from Heaven. You won't have to look very hard because I will surround you with signs in so many different ways. You see, I am limitless when it comes to leaving you signs. Birds, butterflies, silly-shaped rocks, rainbows, clouds that look like me, electronic mishaps, songs on your radio, coins, feathers—oh, I wouldn't begin to tell you how many different kinds of signs that I can bring into your path.

When you see the signs I send, don't let your conscious mind tell you that it wasn't from me because it really was.

Sometimes you may miss the signs that I send you because it is hard to see the beauty in the world around you through tears, and that is okay; I will keep sending signs of love until those tears clear.

The ways you and the family have honored me since I journeyed home to Heaven are pretty amazing. Please try not to dwell on the day and way I passed each day, for the legacy of love I left behind for you is so much more beautiful than my passing. It hurts you to think of my death; that hurt is not the best part of me that I left for you.

I want you to hold on to the sweet memories that we share. So when you find yourself on a day of tears, please replace one of those tears with your favorite memory of me. I will sit with you as you remember me and enjoy the memory with you.

I know you would love to see me in your dreams every night as you sleep. I would love to be there in your dreams each night as well. When you say, "I never see you in my dreams," it places blocks in my way because your energy says you don't see me. I need to help you with that. I want you to change that phrase to "I look forward to seeing you in my dreams at your perfect timing." It will help you to place this positive focus on seeing me in your dreams when the timing is right. I don't come every night in your dreams because you also need space to work through your Grief.

You see, you are gaining more strength through your Grief than you ever knew you could carry in life. Part of that strength is my gift to you, and that gift will only make sense someday when you return home to Heaven here with me. We spend our lives there living for our spiritual growth.

God didn't punish you when I went to Heaven before you. I reached my Soul's beautiful goal of growth in life. I achieved this amazing goal before you, which didn't mean I left you for one moment. Instead, I graduated to the next part of my eternal journey in Heaven.

There will be moments you are incredibly proud of, and there will also be moments you will recognize that you could have handled differently. But the beauty of those moments is that you are living, and not everything will be perfect; that is just part of your growth. None of us can take back the things we could have done differently, but we can grow from those moments. So, of course, telling you this now allows you to look at the days in your future differently so that you will be proud of them when you look back. I didn't have to find a home when I arrived in Heaven because I already had one. You see,

I lived in Heaven before I lived there on Earth with you and returned to my beautiful home in Heaven. You will remember it too when you get here. The colors here in Heaven aren't like anything you have there on Earth!

Remember as you walk through your life every day that I am at your side. I cheer you on in your times of Greatness, and I wipe your tears in your moments of pain.

So what if you have a day of tears? I will stay at your side for comfort. I am most proud of you as you live life to its fullest. It would help if you didn't think that you can no longer live because I am "gone" because I am not gone. Carry me with you in all you do, for I am here. The dreams you wish you could have lived with me are still possible; don't worry, I won't miss them.

My most important message in this letter from Heaven is that I am safe, don't worry about me. I Love you, and am with you always; I want to see you live life to its fullest and catch your dreams. I see you and hear you always, both when you speak out loud and even when you speak silently to me in your mind. Someday this will all make perfect sense when you get to be with me, so don't worry that it doesn't make sense now. Just know that you are a miracle because God made you; because you are a miracle, you can also create miracles.

I Love you...... 🖤 All of my love, me up in Heaven

This is Amanda's final signature. It always included a heart. As you can see, the image may seem out of focus. This is the unfocused view of a bereaved parent.

# CONCLUSION

GRIEVING IS HARD work. You may have to find the help you need, and you have to help yourself. Even though the acute Grief will pass, you now know it will take much longer than you think. You have to believe that your heart will mend but not wholly. You will carry your love for your child forward.

You must believe that you will see your child again. It's the only way to live everyday life with any semblance of normalcy. You must trust that God has a plan and understand that your time on this earth will end. You have no control over when it's your last day. That is a fact. I pray for every parent out there who has suffered a significant loss.

Grief will either make you a better person or cause you to harden your heart as you resist its lessons. A bereaved parent has the opportunity for unparalleled spiritual growth. Strengthening your faith will take time to happen, but you can grow deeply. By learning that life is a precious gift, you can do more than exist; you can live on a higher plane. My grieving produced spiritual growth. You can grow more in a year of grieving than in several years of life with few difficulties.

The death of a loved one can leave you feeling spiritually off balance. You will question God, it shakes your faith, and you may challenge His plan, but allow Him to work mightily in you and give you strength. It becomes overwhelming. You believe that life is not supposed to happen like this. It is natural to have questions when unwanted and unexpected loss comes into your life. To survive your Grief, you must set the questions aside and not let the negative thoughts consume you. You realize that Grief is love, and love gives you the strength to move forward in your child's memory.

## Sorrow will be your companion

One thing about being in Grief is that your sorrow is inevitable, and your loss is so real that you experience it to the depth of your being. So I embraced the sorrow; this process results in strengthened perseverance, character, and hope. But as a bereaved parent, you experience that blow to your heart that you think will never go away. I will tell you that these severe distraught feelings lessen with time.

There are some lessons in life that you only learn through times of Grief or suffering. Your level and length of sorrow define your limitations. After you come out of the shock, trauma, and depression, you learn to embrace the sorrow and return to the world; however, everything radically changes and is rearranged. You rearrange your values. For instance, this world tends to value status, focus on material things, and take pride in one's accomplishments and personal success. You realize these things don't really matter to you.

Unfortunately, self-pity is a dangerous emotion that can slither in and block all your progress toward healing. Being stuck in Grief is complex. I focused so much on my hurt that I became stuck in Grief for many months. My loss became the central focus of my life, dominating my daily existence. My loss became larger than all other relationships. At the time, I was content feeling this way. You sometimes have to learn the hard way. There is no perfect path in one's Grief journey.

## Compassion grows within you

You develop much more compassion for others who are grieving because you feel their pain at the most profound human level. The emotions return as you meet others who have lost a loved one. Everyone is different in handling their Grief. You truly understand that some people want to be left alone, and others want to express their Grief.

Your compassion becomes strong. You are slower to place judgment on other people who unintentionally say hurtful things. You are more willing to approach people who seem down or troubled. You know how to assist others in Grief and understand what to say and what not to say to them. In a sense, you become a qualified griever and can relate to the suffering person. So it's a great opportunity. Now that you have the qualifications, you can effectively help others. You know the grieving process has given you this skill.

When you lose a child, Grief changes you. You will feel completely different and make a 180-degree turn. When you go to a funeral home, you will know what those who have lost are going through; you'll see what you can do to help them. Before your tragic loss, you go through the line, shake hands, and say, "I'm sorry for your loss." You don't really understand. But after you've lost a loved one, you have a different concept of their distress. Now you feel the real pain and sorrow they are experiencing.

When a loved one dies, the week of the funeral is usually hectic—preparing for all the details and obligations. But in the weeks and months that follow, if you are honest, you will be surprised to see those around you resuming their everyday lives. You may ask yourself, "How could they?" Yet you know this is natural. Everyone's life goes on, but you may wonder how you will ever be part of that life again. You cannot merely "turn off" your Grief; you will always carry a part of that Grief with you. But as you walk through your Grief journey, you must take conscious steps forward each day. At some point in time, you will be able to function again in a normal way.

## One life to live

Grief reminds you that you only have one life to live and you need to make it count. You fully understand there are material things that we put too much emphasis on that aren't important at all. Family is necessary, and we take everybody for granted too often.

When you hear people say, "Life is short," the words do not impact you until you experience the death of a loved one. A bereaved parent becomes wiser, more humane, more compassionate, and more fully human after experiencing Grief. In this way, Grief sets you apart. People who have gone through it are different.

When you understand the depth and importance of our world, you begin to value other things—like people. People are the only things going on to eternity. You love your children and family with more passion; you value your friends, neighbors, and new acquaintances more deeply.

## Grief strengthens you

Grief enables you to relate to others at a deeper level than before. Until you've experienced Grief, you cannot truly empathize with someone else who is going through it. During my healing process, I found myself becoming more sensitive to the hurts and needs of others.

Sometimes you can't even recognize the person you were before you lost your loved one. You strengthen your ability to empathize or have compassion. You are less quick to place judgment on a situation or a person. What may appear on the outside to be one way may be a completely different story on the inside. There are always two sides to a story.

Moving forward results in experiencing a lessening of the pain. You start to treasure the best memories of your loved one. You begin to gain the energy to form new relationships and try new things. Of course, the most challenging mountain to climb is realistically accepting the loss of your child. But you learn to accept your loss. Finally, you understand that you can balance joy and sadness as a part of your life.

Although moving forward involves making some hard decisions, there are great rewards to the person who dares to make those decisions. Initially, you never think you can ever be normal again. But the pain eases, and eventually, you dare to move forward.

You gain strength to move on. You acknowledge that things will never be the same again, and you must desire God's plan for your life. Letting go of a lost loved one is tough, especially when the love is deep. Your loved one filled a need in you that is now lost. You have to admit to yourself that your child is gone forever. It isn't easy to acknowledge that life goes on, and you have to get back into life. Acceptance is the most challenging transition during this difficult journey. Releasing is not forgetting; it is the act of setting free. Your loved one was such a blessing to you. Cherish the memories.

## Coming to closure

By now, you have recognized that everyone grieves in different ways and for different amounts of time. Therefore, closure is also an individual experience. Closure in Grief is when a particular struggle, emotion, or problem ends or reaches the point that you are free to move on.

For some people, closure occurs only after a long period. For others, it happens at specific moments. Closure can come through the words or comfort of another person, a crucial memory, a letter, a graveside visit, a Scripture, a new understanding, or a service to another. God will provide a healing closure for you and bless you in that closure. So a bereaved parent will pray for closure and search for it.

Others should never rush a person in the grieving process. It would be best to process your feelings and emotions fully, and you should not feel guilty about taking the necessary time. However, to proceed with healing, there will come a time when you have to say, "Enough." It is time to move forward.

## Good Grief

The most important thing to understand if you are stuck in Grief is that only you can decide to get unstuck. Only you can choose to move on. You may have closed yourself off from interactions in life that generally would be healthy for you. You're so sorrowful that you close out genuinely compassionate people in your world. You start disengaging from life to control your world. But as you disengage, you cut off that life supply and support you desperately need.

Choose to move forward in your Grief—rebuild relationships, serve others in your community, express your emotions, share your story, and begin a new sport, hobby, or activity. Your effort to control your life and cut off relational ties will not help anyone, least of all you.

Think of something good that has happened to you lately. If you do not feel you can label anything as good, think instead of the "exceptions" to your sorrow. Think of those enjoyable minor moments when you did not focus on your sadness. For an instant, you may have felt joy.

The mind can't occupy itself with two thoughts simultaneously. So when I focused on enjoyable, fun, different, and exciting things, the thoughts of sorrow did not seep into my head. Instead, I enjoyed seeing and appreciating all of nature, the bright days of sunlight, the calmness of the rain, and just enjoying the taste of a good meal.

Good Grief is accepting that your loved one has died, carrying the sorrow and pain, and knowing there is more to come. Good Grief is getting through the days, the months, and, eventually, the years. It is critical to manage your negative thoughts through that first year. After that, the intense, uncontrollable emotions will run their course. It would help if you believed you would see sunshine again, even during those cloudy days.

The day will come when you discover that you can make it without your child. This traumatic loss will change you. Grief takes time, but you will find it gets better, and you must recognize that it is a period of transition to a brand new kind of life for you.

Grief is a process and a series of actions and involves forward movement—going from one emotion, one level, one day, to the next. There is such a thing as good Grief. It consists of identifying the loss, recognizing the grieving process, accepting that life will never be the same, and continuing the journey. There is also complicated Grief: continually thinking about the person who died and refusing to let them go. Counseling will you help you deal with those longing feelings.

## Suicide thoughts are Taboo

A bereaved parent may feel so distraught and lost that there may be suicidal thoughts. The Grief can be so intense that you cannot live with this tragedy. You want to die to relieve the severe, indescribable pain. You want to reunite with your loved one. It is vital to seek help from a professional if you think of acting on these thoughts.

It all becomes uncomfortable sometimes, but you must get beyond those feelings and ask others for the help you need. Another way to seek help is through a grief recovery support group. In this setting, you can find people who will be concerned friends, who will not worry about the "right" words to say or the "best" way to respond to you. Instead, they will accept you, love you, and not have expectations.

This Grief can be very deep-seated. God knows your sorrow; no matter how dark or painful your situation is, Jesus can bring you hope. Yet sometimes, you feel like rejecting that hope and embracing your despair. Instead, it is vital to stay resilient and gain strength to help ourselves and to help others in need.

## Saying Goodbye

It is difficult to say goodbye. I have never said goodbye to my daughter. She will always be with me in spirit, so not saying goodbye is my way of keeping her in my thoughts and memories. Saying goodbye is not a one-time action. It is a process with many different and complicated steps. It is okay if you don't feel ready for this now. Understand that saying goodbye occurs gradually over time. That time may not come if that is your desire.

I say goodbye to you, my reader. Thank you for reading my book. Many bereaved parents are hurting every day. My goal in publishing this book is to leave a legacy for my daughter and help those who have lost a child, companion, family member, spouse, or significant other with their Grief.

You can help. I would be honored if you could take a few moments and write a short review of my book *No Greater Pain* and leave it on Amazon. You can find my book on Amazon by entering the title and proceeding to "Customer Reviews." Your review is important to me. Heartfelt thoughts will help reach others who are struggling with Grief.

Thank you for considering writing a review. I intend to read each one and offer my sincerest thanks.

My warmest regards,

Ronald J. Ross

# READINGS TO CONSIDER

THESE BOOKS WILL be helpful for any bereaved parent. These are the books I have read. They helped me manage Grief through this most difficult time.

*Shattered – Surviving the loss of a child*: Gary Roe
*The worst loss – How families have healed from the death of a child:* Barbara D, Rosof
*It's OK that you're not OK:* Megan Devine
*Imagine Heaven:* John Burke
*90 minutes in Heaven:* Don Piper
*Bearing the unbearable*: Joanne Cacciatore, Ph.D.
*The grieving brain*: Mary-Frances O'Connor, Ph.D.
*Beyond tears – Living after losing a child*: Ellen Mitchell
*Grieving dads – To the brink and back:* Kelly Farley and David Dicole
*I wasn't ready to say goodbye:* Brook Noel and Pamela Blair, PhD
*How to survive the loss of a child*: Catherine M Sanders PhD
*Comfort for the parents' grieving hearts:* Gary Roe
*Journeying through Grief:* Kenneth C Haugk
*My journey through Grief into grace:* Kathleen B. Duncan
*How to go on living when someone you love dies:* Therese A, Rando, Ph.D.

# ABOUT ME – THE AUTHOR

The pain of losing a child is only compounded by the crushing weight of knowing you have to live the rest of your life without them. In author Ronald Ross' debut, No Greater Pain, he speaks to parents everywhere who have suffered the devastating grief of losing a child.

Ron is proud to share his vulnerable feelings about losing his daughter and desires to help others who have suffered a similar significant loss through his personal experience, readings, and research.

Ron was born in Pittsburgh, Pennsylvania, and follows the Christian Faith. He enjoys playing tennis and golf, engaging in family activities, visiting the appealing national parks in Maryland, and following his favorite sports teams.

Ronald Ross worked in Government for 30+ years. Now retired, his traumatic grief experience led him to appreciate so much more in life, especially his children. Five live on this earth, and one now lives in Heaven.

# ACKNOWLEDGMENTS

First and foremost, I want to acknowledge my wife, Elaine, for her emotional support during my challenging journey. Many thanks for her feedback and input as I penned this journey. A loving wife, she helped our family and me in so many ways; my appreciation for her is absolute.

I appreciate my son, who became stronger than I could have imagined; his compassion and support for me are permanently etched in my memory. He and his wife gave me the space I needed throughout the first year. My younger daughter grieved with me and provided more support than she realized. Her Faith in healing from her sister's death was admirable.

I want to recognize my three step-children for their understanding and compassion during the most challenging times. Special appreciation to my stepdaughter and her husband for their emotional support —and time, for her mother and me.

My two sisters provided sympathetic listening ears; my brother showed more understanding than imaginable with his heartfelt emotions expressing his love and compassion for our entire family.

I acknowledge my special friends, who shared their own tragedies and compassion. They helped me understand the uncontrollable emotions of losing a child and gave me the resilience to look to the future, keeping memories of my daughter close.

Good friends stay with you during difficult, uncomfortable times. A special thanks to my close friend, Jim, who not only supported me during extreme times of despair but wrote and recorded a song in memory of my daughter.

Many thanks to my tennis buddies for keeping me involved in activities, inviting me to breakfasts and dinners, and providing brief respites from the hurt.

I acknowledge my former wife (Amanda's mother) and her husband. Sometimes, death brings families together in Grief, and I thank them for their conversations as we shared our pain. In addition, a longtime friend, Sharon, has supported our mutual families in many kindhearted ways.

When emotions ran high, my Father-in-law provided more love and emotional support than a son-in-law could imagine; he has always been like a father to me. My in-laws have been married for over 72 years and are most caring and compassionate.

I thank all my friends and acquaintances not mentioned here for your phone calls, cards, texts, emails, and thoughtful gifts you provided at the times when I needed them most.

Finally, my warmest thank you to Dr. Vonda for professionally editing my manuscript before publication and providing consoling comments.

CPSIA information can be obtained
at www.ICGtesting.com
Printed in the USA
LVHW040306200523
747574LV00005B/309

9 798822 908604